Dr. Bodo Roedel
In collaboration with
Nadja Gaertel and Susen Werner

Aikido - The Basics
Techniques, Principles, Concept

ikkyo omote waza

Meyer & Meyer Sport

Original title: Aikido Grundlagen
© Meyer & Meyer Verlag, 2009

British Library Cataloguing in Publication Data
A catalogue record for this book is available from the British Library

Bodo Roedel
Aikido – The Basics
Maidenhead: Meyer & Meyer (UK) Ltd., 2011
ISBN: 978-1-84126-302-1

© 2011 by Meyer & Meyer (UK) Ltd.
Auckland, Beirut, Budapest, Cairo, Cape Town, Dubai, Graz, Indianapolis,
Maidenhead, Melbourne, Olten, Singapore, Tehran, Toronto
Member of the World
Sport Publishers' Association (WSPA)
www.w-s-p-a.org
Printed and bound by: B.O.S.S Druck und Medien GmbH
ISBN: 978-1-84126-302-1
E-Mail: info@m-m-sports.com
www.m-m-sports.com

Contents

The Reason for a Book About Aikido

The initial thoughts about this book occurred in 2007 during one of Christian Tissier's sensei summer seminars on the side of a swimming pool in the Côte d'Azur. Contributing to the first reflections regarding the content of the book were Nadja Gaertel, Martina Dorka, Susen Werner and Dieter Becker.

When we asked ourselves what a book about the basics of Aikido should contain, we soon were all absolutely agreed that it should not only contain the basic knowledge of the techniques that a beginner in Aikido would particularly need – for example foot movements, forward rolls etc and the details of the techniques – but that there should also be something about the background of the concept of Aikido.

The dictionary defines **concept** as a clearly derived general idea or a plan. The book should also cover, in a clear form, just which plan is applicable to Aikido. This should be based on thoughts that have been developed, bit-by-bit, so that they are therefore clearly understandable and executable by everyone.

As a result, this book has three aims. First of all, it is there to support those who have set out on the road to learning Aikido. Secondly, maybe it can also provide inspiration to those who have been devoting themselves to the art and have been practicing Aikido for some time already. Throughout the book, you will find frequent references as to why there are various different styles in Aikido. The main reason for this (in my opinion) does not lie in the various technical details – this is only the case on first sight. A much deeper reason lies in the differences of concept in the various styles, irrespective of whether they are formulated explicitly or only implicitly – or, in the worst case, not even known about by pupils and their instructors.

In other words, it is precisely the conceptual background that determines the different styles in Aikido. Each style can well be consistent and more or less built up logically and still remain executable. If you look at the underlying concept, there is no longer a question of whether this or that technique functions well, but a question of what opportunities for development exist on the basis of each concept. In Aikido, when you look at the various considerations in this aspect, then you will find considerable differences in quality.

At this point, I don't wish to hide the fact that my own heart reaches out for a concept in Aikido that fulfills at least three demands:

- It exists (something that doesn't always immediately go without saying) and can be formulated and checked.

- It is logical (i.e., is consistent within itself) and executable.

- It lends itself to Aikido as a demanding form of Martial Art and the art of movement.

As a third aim I also hope that this book will provide interesting suggestions for lessons carried out by Aikido instructors.

For every instructor there should be two questions regarding the main emphasis in the development of one's own Aikido. "What do I do?" and "Why am I doing it this way?" Because there is no competition in Aikido, these two questions are absolutely central for an interesting Aikido training session. The criterion that differentiates the pro from the layman is when an instructor can provide answers to these questions. Nobody would let someone else repair his automobile if he couldn't give an answer to these two questions. It is the same in educational theory: The pro is distinguishable from the layman by using his actions in a reflective and explanative manner – i.e., when he can answer the two questions referred to earlier. Therefore why shouldn't we also demand this of an Aikido instructor, because after all every Martial Art is also a form of education – but more on this later.

In light of the examination of the conceptual background, (hopefully) it will become clear that Aikido instruction concerns the application of both intelligent didactics (What is being instructed?) and method (How is it being instructed?), especially when one wants to go deeply into the subject of Aikido. If the Aikido instruction is limited to demonstrating and copying, then the principles of Aikido will remain unknown to many. Otherwise, Aikido would seem to be merely a collection of tricks and appear as more or less elegantly executed movements – and many opportunities of developing it further would become lost.

From this point of view, it is no coincidence that the basic thoughts for this book emerged during one of Christian Tissier's sensei courses, because he is not only a master of the techniques but also a master of Aikido didactics and method.

Like no other, he is always able to see the principles behind Aikido from new angles, and thus allows his pupils the possibility of recognizing and understanding them. I owe him my special thanks, because, without his instruction, my own development in exercising Aikido both as a pupil of his and as an instructor would not be so complete.

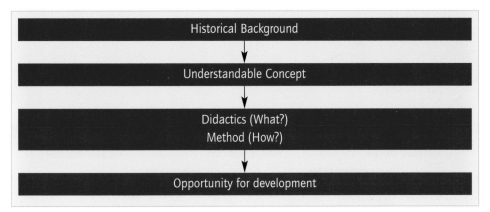

Aikido, as it can be taught today and as it is described in this book, is based on links between these points.

A book about the basics of Aikido must contain numerous technical details. But because of obvious limitations, it cannot cover all the interesting technical aspects of the art. The aspects that I have included have been chosen because I believe they are particularly worthy of mention and that they usefully support the learning and teaching process for the person practicing Aikido. Along with the main emphasis of the chosen selection, there will always be a reduction of the Aikido techniques that can be covered in such a book. Of course, I could have chosen to construct it differently, so there can be no claim to raise any objections regarding exclusivity or completeness. Naturally, a book about the art of movement reaches its limits when it comes to expressing feeling for movement in the techniques – because, unfortunately, feelings in the medium of a book can only be described and not pictured or illustrated. I, also, could not resolve this paradox.

The following have acted as training partners in this book:

Martina Dorka

Nadja Gaertel

Targan Kursun

Thomas Puetz

Susen Werner

I owe them hearty thanks for their efforts and patience.

The photographs on pages 15, 24, 31 and 327 were taken by Maria Polevaya. Those on pages 17, 29, 91, 237, 241 and 329 by Marc Schroeder. For the use of these photos may I also give my thanks. The photograph on page 325 is by Dr. Bodo Roedel. All the other photos were taken by Iris Pohl (www.iris-pohl.de).

My particular thanks goes to Nadja Gaertel for providing Chapter 1.1 and for her intensive work in editing the whole text in the book. Similarly, thanks go to Susen Werner who wrote and illustrated Chapter 9.1.

Dr. Bodo Roedel

Foreword by Christian Tissier shihan, 7th dan aikikai

I know Bodo Roedel as a considerate, reliable man who is always loyal to our common interest and me. He, therefore, has the necessary characteristics that allow a pupil to look forward to many years of training without worrying about achieving a direct aim - or rather I should say they look forward to cherishing the continual repetition of the 'moment'. Always attentive, he returns untiringly from the headway we have made together to go on and discover new things.

To take on a young man, to teach him firstly the basics and then the finer points of Aikido, to watch him as he develops into a fine person capable of passing on his knowledge – this was an experience that was important to me and makes one very aware of one's own position and responsibility.

Passing on knowledge is an exchange process. This exchange process opened up new horizons for me and inspired me: I thank him for this – I thank all my pupils similarly. The spontaneous discussion and the justified questions that came as well as the thoughts that led to this book are all evidence of the variety and the many possible viewpoints surrounding this subject.

The ability required for its achievement is equally various. Bodo Roedel possesses very many of these abilities and it is surely also the case that he has called on his knowledge from his background as a Doctor of Education for his book. I wish him all success with this book.

Christian Tissier

Notes About the Content of the Book

The book has nine chapters with the following content:

Chapter 1: This chapter describes what constitutes Aikido and how Aikido is defined. Aikido is also explained in contrast to other sporting Martial Arts forms. This section of the chapter was written by Nadja Gaertel.

Chapter 2: The basic foot movements are covered. These appear continually in all Aikido techniques i.e., when one knows the basic foot techniques, one can understand and learn new techniques more rapidly. Therefore, the foot movements are shown as movements with an exercise partner. Similarly, the relationship of Aikido with the movements of a sword is compared.

Chapter 3: This chapter covers the most important hand movements required in Aikido. Just like the foot movements, certain hand and arm movements are continuously being mentioned in Aikido. It is interesting to look at these in isolation in order to understand the structure of Aikido techniques.

Chapter 4: The so-called 'working up' of the Aikido techniques ('Working on the construction' or 'Working on one's own form') is a considerably important element in the learning process for Aikido. Chapter 4 explains the meaning behind this. Numerous examples are given.

Chapter 5: This chapter includes important details of all the basic techniques. The details should help one to understand the techniques more easily and simplify learning Aikido.

Chapter 6: All Aikido techniques are based on the same principles. While in Chapter 5 the specific technical details were described, the 'metalevel' of techniques in Aikido can be addressed.

Chapter 7: Chapter 7 describes the learning process in Aikido with, in particular, the roles of defender and attacker being covered. In Aikido there is a certain number of basic techniques. These basic techniques are always learnt with identical follow-on sequences.

Chapter 8: It is not only the person carrying out an Aikido technique that learns – the attacker also learns at the same time. Because both of them exercise together constructively, they are dependent on each other for the developments they make. For this reason, this chapter is devoted to the most important elements in the learning process for the attacker.

Chapter 9: Here you will find additional information about Aikido and Aikido training rounding off the book. Susen Werner wrote Section 9.1 in this chapter.

So that reading the text is made as fluid as possible, the person practicing Aikido is shown as *'Aikido-ka'* (covering both male and female). The techniques and attacks are labeled with their Japanese names to avoid difficult translations. You will find the terms and their meanings either directly in the text or in a glossary at the end of the book (see Page 334). The attacker is called *Uke* (from the Japanese verb *ukeru* = to receive i.e., Uke is the person who receives the technique). The defender is called *Tori* (from the Japanese verb *toru* = to take, seize, catch).

The reader should note that perspective in the photos has been changed in part for the various movement sequences in order to illustrate certain details better.

Christian Tissier and Bodo Roedel – irimi nage

"Art is not a thing – it is a way."

Elbert Hubbard

1   What is Aikido?

- What do the characters *"ai-ki-do"* mean?

- What is the viewpoint of this book regarding explanation of the basics in Aikido?

- How does Aikido compare to other Martial Arts and sports?

According to the way that any *Aikido-ka* tries to examine Aikido, an answer to the question of what Aikido is all about is always varied. In other words, it is difficult to give a generally final definition of Aikido that everyone can really agree with. Perhaps there are as many definitions of Aikido as there are people practicing Aikido, because, of course, each individual can have his own personal viewpoint.

In the following passages are several possible ways of looking at Aikido. Later in the book we will survey, time and again, the various aspects of this more deeply and in greater detail.

For the onlooker, Aikido is an array of highly developed and effective techniques for self-defense.

The term - "highly developed" - means that lifts and levers are cleverly used in order to achieve the maximum effect with the least effort.

All the techniques are based on the same principles (see Chapter 6). The basis of Aikido is founded on natural and simple movements – thus, anyone can learn Aikido. In this context, "natural" means that the movements are all executed in a radius about the body that the *Aikido-ka* determines and is similar to that which he is used to in daily life. In this perspective, the aim of Aikido training is to continually improve the execution of the techniques. Work topics are:

- relaxed movement,

- learning to do flowing movements,

- exercising hard and appropriately schooling the leg muscles, and

- using the hands and arms correctly.

"Internally", Aikido is a method to be worked up by oneself. This includes, for example, exercising:

- the concentration,
- staying power,
- the ability to assert oneself,
- the ability to cooperate as well as...
- ...self confidence

The first perspective shows that Aikido is all about the art of movement – one can truly call Aikido a 'sport'. Aikido differs from techniques of meditation like e.g., *zen*, even though Aikido possesses meditative elements (see Page 329).

The second perspective illustrates that Aikido offers the possibility to practice one's mental senses – in the broadest sense, Aikido here is a method of developing the personality. Both of these perspectives are, of course, mutually conditional on each other. The internal state of mind influences the movement and vice versa. This is also an explanation for the literal term 'fighting art' (martial art). Inter alia, the term 'art' means that the external movements reflect the internal state and this is what is expressed by the *Aikido-ka* – similar to recognizing the expression achieved by a painter in a work of art. Of course, the point mentioned above concerning the mental senses can be found in many types of sport.

If one takes a perspective beyond the first and second ones, one can begin to get close to the nature of Aikido, because the first two alone do not suffice as a full explanation. Aikido gives one the opportunity to work together constructively with other people and to try to carry out an exchange – in this sense Aikido is a form of intensive communication. One could almost call it 'body dialogue'.

This makes it clear how Aikido differs from other types of sport and in particular from other forms of martial art. After all, Aikido is the only martial art where anyone who is practicing it accepts that 50% of the time they will lose the bout, and despite this, they will use the experience to make progress for themselves and others.

Because, in Aikido, there are always at least two people exercising together, one can also think about Aikido from an ethical perspective. With this in mind, one can try to answer the questions "What should I do?" and "How should I proceed?"

In Aikido there is an easy answer for this: "Defend yourself when you are being attacked – however, also call on the attacker to stop his actions in time before you injure him. React to the movements accordingly and don't cause more injury than is absolutely necessary so that you, yourself, remain unhurt."

If you look at the Japanese word "Aikido" in an etymological dictionary, you will find the following definition:

The syllable *"ai"* means 'joining', 'unifying', 'harmonizing'. Sometimes *"ai"* is translated as 'love'. The syllable *"ki"* means 'feeling', 'purpose', 'spirit', 'life energy' (see Page 22) and the syllable *"do"* approximates 'way' – in the sense of a process one has to go through in order to achieve physical and mental development. Thus, the meaning of the combined first two syllables is "to unite opposite intentions or powers in harmony". Therefore, one possible translation of Aikido could be: the way or the method of uniting (opposite) powers in harmony.

Japanese characters for ai-ki-do

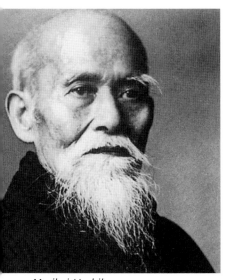

Morihei Ueshiba

When all is said and done, one can approach the question of what Aikido is by having a look at the history of Aikido. Seen from an historical perspective, Aikido is a classical Japanese martial art – so-called *Budo* - like, for example also *Judo* or *Karate-do*. It was created in the 20th Century by the Japanese Morihei Ueshiba (1883-1969) as a synthesis of various martial arts (see Page 322).

The historical heart of Aikido, therefore, lies in the long tradition of Japanese martial arts. In the meanwhile, Aikido has spread across the world and other cultures have influenced it. This is also a reason why Aikido has developed in various different directions and is continuing to be developed.

What is Aikido? A few common perspectives			
Onlooker's Perspective	Internal Perspective	Higher Perspective	Historical Perspective
Self-defense	Concentration	Communication	Classic *Budo*
Martial Art	Self-confidence	Dialogue	Historical Traditions
Art of Movement	Development of the Personality	Exchange	Further Modern Development
Sport	Technique as a Method of Internal Work	Learning with each other- Against each other	Different styles
Life Form/Ethics – Education - Self-development			

What is ki?

The elements of the *"ai"* and *"do"* in the word Aikido are relatively easily explained. The *"ki"* syllable in the word needs some further mention, as there is much scope for more interpretation here. Generally, *"ki"* is (as seen from a Far Eastern viewpoint) translated as 'feeling', 'purpose/intention', 'life energy' or 'vitality'. The Chinese for it is *"chi"* (as in *tai chi* – the Chinese Art of Movement); the Indian word for it is *prana*. In particular, the Chinese version refers to a concept of flowing energy and forces, as used in Chinese traditional medicine.

The source of *"ki"* is a point just below the navel – the so-called *kikai-tanden* or *hara*. Literally translated it means the "sea of energy". Every person has access to his *"ki"*. Differences in the strength of the life energy or vitality and the ability to use *"ki"* exist when blockages or tension obstruct the flow of *"ki"* through the body. Traditional Chinese medicine therefore sees this state as a cause of illness.

Some *Aikido-ka* bring their interpretation of life energy so far as to literally want to let their *"ki"* flow and attempt to 'let it out' of the body – this would then akin it to an effective force.

For Aikido pupils from Western countries, it is easier to understand (and at the same time appear less esoteric) if "ki" is defined by using the following: The ability to assert oneself, determination, willpower, motivation and self-efficacy. The *Aikido-ka* exercises these qualities when he is training and embeds them into his techniques. "ki" is also closely associated with words such as intention/purpose, decision and action (see Chapter 6.8).

Of course, the idea of 'flowing energy' can also be simply illustrated. Imagining that *"ki"* flows like water through our arms can supplement relaxation, because such a flow is only possible when our arms and joints are 'loosened up' i.e., relaxed. Similarly a full water hose is not slack. This image may also help to allow you to work up the correct feeling for a movement. To let your *"ki"* 'flow', means nothing less than being able to move naturally with the right balance between relaxation and tension.

1.1   Aikido Comparisons

One can get closer to the essence of Aikido by comparing it further with other sporting martial arts forms. This is not a question of trying to decide which martial arts form is 'better' or 'more effective', but rather - by making the differences clear - to show where the special features of Aikido lie and how its relationship measures up with the other sporting martial arts forms.

When an *Aikido-ka* tells someone that he is practicing Aikido, the first thing he is asked is what Aikido actually is. This is usually followed by the question: "Is it something like *Judo* or *Karate*?" Because other forms of martial arts are better known about than Aikido, those coming into contact with Aikido or hearing about it for the first time often try to sort it in their minds into a system known already to them.

Compared with Aikido and its further spread around the world, the greater knowledge of other sporting forms of the martial arts can be attributed to the fact that there is no competitive form of Aikido. Accordingly, no championships are carried out and also Aikido is not an Olympic sport and therefore not talked about much in the media. Besides this, in Aikido (at first sight) there are no sensational techniques to draw wide audiences (compare the 'breaking' techniques in *Karate* or *Taekwondo*).

Western forms of martial arts, such as boxing, wrestling or fencing, distinguish themselves from the origins of the Asian martial arts that are strongly linked to philosophical traditions and specific spiritual attitudes. Although there are parallels in technique between the far-eastern and western sports in martial arts, e.g., between *Karate* and Savate-Boxe Française, or between *Ju-Jutsu* and the medieval self-defense methods, they are essentially not comparable. The original aim of the Asian *Budo* – in contrast to western fighting sports – is not (only) victory over the opponent, but (also) conquering oneself. This way, the actual sense of exercising for a long time is about reaching a level of self-realization in the course of exercise. By exercising to reach the external purpose, the exercise should lead onto the internal feeling. By practicing certain techniques, the attention is also to be directed inwards, thus making the automated overall cycle of a movement a mirror of the inner attitude.

Karsten Prause 4th dan aikikai and Bodo Roedel – Aikido demonstration during the summer course run by Christian Tissier in Exertal, Germany 2007.

Accordingly, it is more appropriate to describe far-Eastern methods as martial "arts" rather than martial "sports" – although both terms are frequently used as synonyms. When comparing Aikido with other far-Eastern martial arts, what becomes particularly apparent are the differences in technique.

Judo

Judo was developed from the relatively older *Ju-Jutsu* that dates back to the fighting methods of the Japanese Samurai. The word *Judo* is made up from *'ju'* meaning 'to yield' and *'do'* meaning 'way'. Together they mean 'way of softness' or 'way of yielding'. *Judo*, as practiced today, was created by Jigoro Kano (1860-1938) and it excluded all the injurious techniques in *Ju-Jutsu* and allowed the possibility of submitting during a fight. Today, *Judo* is the martial art best known about. *Judo* has been an Olympic event since 1964.

In *Judo* there are standing techniques but also a number of groundwork techniques done kneeling or lying down. The partner is brought under control by using throws, holds, strangling actions and levers. Differently to Aikido, *Judo* techniques generally require gripping one another's jacket, thus making the attacks less dynamic. By having to grip the jacket, Tori and Uke are often in a position much closer to each other than in Aikido.

The development of *Ju-Jutsu* into *Judo* is an example of how a system has been changed into a method of internal work – *'do'*, while originally the only aim was to injure and kill – *jutsu*. The same development has occurred in the way the history of Aikido has come on. It was Morihei Ueshiba, the creator of Aikido, who transformed the *daito ryu aiki-jujitsu* techniques, that had the aim only of defeating the opponent as quickly as possible, into the comparatively softer techniques of the *'do'* (see Chapter 9.4).

Ju-Jutsu

Ju-Jutsu, also known as *Ju-Jitsu*, *Jujitsu* or *Jiu-Jitsu*, is a collective name for Japanese martial art styles including unarmed and armed techniques. It evolved among the Samurai of feudal Japan as a method for defeating an armed and armored opponent with weapons. The word can be broken down into two parts. "Ju" is a concept. The idea behind this meaning of Ju is "to be gentle", "to give away", "to yield", "to blend", "to move out of harm's way". "Jutsu" is the principle or "the action" part of Ju-Jutsu. In Japanese this word means science or technique.

There are many variations of *Ju-Jutsu*, which leads to a diversity of approaches. The methods of combat may include striking (kicking and punching), throwing (body throws, unbalance throws) and restraining (pinning, strangulating, grappling, wrestling). Defense tactics include blocking, evading, off-balancing, blending and escaping. In addition, many schools teach the use of weapons. Modern *Ju-Jutsu* traditions were founded at the end of the 19th Century, when more than 2000 schools of *Ju-Jutsu* existed in Japan. Over time *Ju-Jutsu* has been embraced by law enforcement officials worldwide and continues to be the foundation for many specialized systems used by police.

There are many forms of sport *Ju-Jutsu*. One of the most common is mixed-style competitions, where competitors apply a variety of strikes, throws, and holds to score points. There are also *kata* competitions, where competitors of the same style perform techniques and are judged on their performance. Freestyle competitions also exist, where competitors take turns attacking each other, and the defender is judged on performance.

Karate

Karate-do ('te' = hand, 'kara' = empty giving − "way of the empty hand") can be traced back over centuries of history. The Japanese styles of Karate were created on Okinawa − a group of islands lying to the south of Japan. The most common form of *Karate* today, is the style of *Shotokan Karate* that was created by the founder of modern *Karate*, Gishin Funakoshi. The IOC (International Olympic Committee) Congress recognizes *Karate* as an Olympic sport.

In *Karate*, the fists, edges of the hands, elbows, underarms, feet and knees are predominantly used. Both attack and defense techniques are practiced. In contrast to Aikido, in *Karate*, movements are made almost always in a straight line i.e., direct movements. Partners do not move harmoniously together, but rather try to get through to the opponent in a contest as quickly as possible. In *Shotokan Karate* competitions, punches and kicks are only intimated so that no actual strike is achieved − this would even constitute an offence if done. However, there are styles of *Karate* in which full body contact is used e.g., *Kyokushinkai Karate*.

Taekwondo

Taekwondo is a Korean system of self-defense that has developed on its own over many hundreds of years. In Korea, *Taekwondo* is not counted, however, as a martial art but rather as a type of sport. The term *Taekwondo* is made up of the elements 'tae' = foot, 'kwon' = fist and 'do' = way. Translated, *Taekwondo* means "the art of fighting with the feet and hands". *Taekwondo* has been an Olympic sport since 2000.

In *Taekwondo*, in particular, you use the hands, fingers, fists, knuckles, elbows, knees, feet and head to punch, kick or ram with. Besides mastering the movement sequences and freestyle forms, you also have the 'breaking test', just like in *Karate*. In contrast to other martial arts, in *Taekwondo* the foot techniques are dominant. A fundamental difference to Shotokan *Karate* is furthermore that there are both semi-contact and full body contact fights that can lead to a knockout situation.

Putting these considerations into perspective, the following diagram will appear:

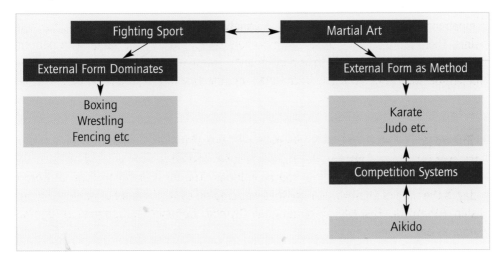

Of course, this form of exact diagram only serves as an aid to make it clear where Aikido has its place. As muted already at the beginning, fighting sports contain elements of the martial arts while, vice versa, martial arts necessarily include elements of sports. Of course, in the martial arts of competitive *Karate* and *Judo* systems, laid down forms – the *kata* - are often practiced outside the contest situation.

Further 'classical' martial arts forms are:

- *Kendo* – a fencing art using a sword made from bamboo (shinai) and stemming from Japan – (*'ken'* = sword)

- *Kyudo* – the way of archery

- *Iaido* – the art of drawing a sword

1.2　The Basic Premises in this Book

In the first chapter we showed some possibilities how one can understand the subject of Aikido better. In the following passages we will continue with a list of the premises valid for this book. The premises of **"Aikido – The Basics"** are oriented on the worldwide mainstream of Aikido. The mainstream is as found in its institutionally historic form under the worldwide umbrella foundation *aiki-kai* and is along the lines of the creator of Aikido – *o-sensei* Morihei Ueshiba.

- Aikido is a martial art and is based on the logical form of the martial arts. Aikido is not a fighting sport (even though it contains sporting elements) i.e., the result of the actions does not count *('jutsu')*. It is rather more to do with the way the result was achieved *('do')*.

- The primary aim is not the application of the Aikido techniques in 'realistic' situations, however, within the sense of a martial art, it is the real functionality of the Aikido techniques that is taken into account. This means that from at least the perspective of the *Aikido-ka*, he should be able to execute his techniques also with a non-*Aikido-ka*. Techniques that do not contain this element of realism are seen as exercises.

- The Aikido techniques are based on standardized principles (see Chapter 6). Conversely, this means that the techniques only function when the principles are observed.

- The use of the modern didactic method of teaching Aikido makes it understandable by everyone (see Chapter 7). This then offers the possibility of a life-long learning process with lots of opportunities for development. ,

- Aikido ranges between the 'ancient' and the 'modern' and is being continually developed further. However, the 'hard core' of Aikido is firmly manifested in its basic techniques.

- The key to understanding Aikido lies in exercise and training.

- The Aikido techniques count at the same time as a method for the 'mental work' to be done by the *Aikido-ka*. As a result, there is not only a form of Aikido that is oriented round the technique, but contrary to this also a form of Aikido where the mental work comes to the fore. Moreover, without the correct technique there can be no Aikido! The technique and the mental work are the two sides of a coin.

Christian Tissier and Bodo Roedel – kokyu nage

1.3   Aikido Exercise Forms

In Aikido there are various forms of exercises that are dependent on which subject is to be learned. These exercise forms are independent from the particular technique. In the *tachi waza* techniques both Uke and Tori are in the standing position. In the *hanmi handachi waza* techniques Tori is kneeling (see Chapter 2.9) and is attacked by Uke from a standing position. Uke's aim is then to prevent Tori from standing up. If Tori and Uke are exercising *suwari waza* then this means that both do this from a kneeling position.

Ju no geiko indicates a soft form of practicing where Uke rides with the movement offering no resistance – this form is mainly about learning the technique. On the other hand *go no keiko* indicates a form of practice carried out firmly and with force i.e., Tori must already be able to execute the technique to be practiced well.

If Uke attacks Tori always with the same form, and the latter reacts freely with various different techniques each time, then we speak about *jiyu waza*. The term *randori* indicates that Uke uses a free attack and Tori reacts with different techniques.

Randori also indicates defense against a number of 'Uke' who usually attack with *ryo kata dori* (see Page 278).

The term *kokyu-ho* indicates exercises that explicitly illustrate the principle of communicative exchange (see Chapter 6.3). They are not techniques *(waza)* but are exercises *(ho)*.

Weapons in Aikido

Tori can be attacked by Uke holding a weapon. In *tanto dori*, Uke attacks with a knife and therefore Tori's aim is to defend against the attack and take the knife away from Uke (see Chapter 5.5). In *tachi-dori*, Uke attacks with a (wooden) sword and using a technique Tori takes it away from him. *Jo dori* indicates that Uke attacks with a stick (staff) and Tori takes it away from him. Conversely, in *jo nage waza*, Tori is holding a stick and Uke attacks him by grabbing hold of the *jo* – that he then uses to defend himself.

Besides these, there are Aikido exercises in which Uke as well as Tori have either a sword or a stick.

Kumi jo indicates partners exercising with the stick – *kumi tachi* is partners exercising with a sword.

Uke and Tori go on to practice laid down sequences of movements – so-called *kata* – that would be far too dangerous to use in free training. Similar to the Aikido exercises without weapons, the level of intensity in the attack and in defense increases according to the caliber of the *Aikido-ka*.

Practicing with weapons in Aikido makes sense as follows: For one, the creator of Aikido, Morihei Ueshiba learned to use various weapon techniques himself including exercises with the sword, stick, lance etc. So, exercises with the stick and the sword are part of the historical heart of Aikido.

However, the following aspects are possibly more interesting: Practicing with weapons serves to let the *Aikido-ka* understand several aspects. In Aikido, with or without weapons, the movements of the feet are the same or very similar. The same applies to the hand movements. Additionally, many Aikido techniques without weapons are executed with the feeling of a cutting or stabbing movement (not pulling or pushing) and this is identical to the work with the sword.

Besides, one gets to understand the distance between Uke and Tori better by practicing with the sword, because the weapon automatically determines this. In part, working with a weapon is eventually direct and rapid – practicing using the *jo* or *bokken* therefore helps to develop the martial arts character of Aikido further.

Christian Tissier and Bodo Roedel – 2007 – practicing using the wooden sword – bokken

Further Reading:
"The Book of Five Rings" by Miyamoto Musashi circa 1645 – Translated by various

"A good hockey player plays where the puck is. A great hockey player plays where the puck is going to be."

Wayne Gretzky

2 Foot Movements

- What do you begin doing in Aikido?
- How do you move your feet in Aikido?
- What do the foot movements look like?

As a martial art, Aikido is an art of moving. This means that correct and sure foot movements in Aikido are particularly important in order to be able to execute the techniques. Invariably, therefore, the foot movements take priority over hand movements. When the *Aikido-ka* has managed to master the foot movements, then he can equally easily learn the hand and arm movements – in short – the hand movements always follow the foot movements and not vice versa.

We will, therefore, introduce all the basic foot movements used in Aikido in this chapter. Because Aikido is based on standardized principles, there are a series of foot movements that always crop up. If one has understood these, then just beginners in Aikido can discover the basic techniques more easily. Each foot movement is covered in this chapter using examples of the movement to make them clear. The examples of the movements are, on the other hand, only part movements of the Aikido techniques.

Because the positions of the feet in Aikido are identical to the positions with the sword (see Chapter 2.10), three of the positions with the sword (amongst others) serve as illustration to allow a better understanding of the foot movements.

The foot movements in Aikido always follow a prioritized pattern that is the same for all Aikido basic techniques:

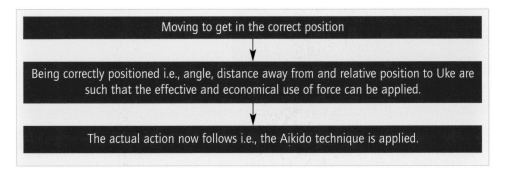

Moving to get in the correct position

↓

Being correctly positioned i.e., angle, distance away from and relative position to Uke are such that the effective and economical use of force can be applied.

↓

The actual action now follows i.e., the Aikido technique is applied.

Thus, Tori just doesn't simply move, he always moves with the aim of being in a better position than before (see the execution along the principle of simple movements in Chapter 6.6).

2.1 kamae

We first have a closer look at the basic position – the on guard position – the Japanese term for this is *kamae*. There is no specific on guard position in Aikido. The feet are simply placed one behind the other along a straight line. The rear foot is pointing in the forward direction, just like normal walking. The picture shows the position from the front.

The on guard position in Aikido as seen from the side.

When one starts Aikido, it is very important to learn to adopt a stable and low down stance. At the beginning, this means that you have to train your leg muscles for the specific Aikido stresses. On this, note that the feet are behind each other at a greater distance apart than they would be normally.

The leading foot is slightly turned outwards in order to obtain more stability. The front knee is well bent so that it is just over the toes. The knee always points in the same direction as the foot.

The rear leg is stretched out and the bottom is tensed so that you are not standing with a hollow back.

By pulling the leading foot back in a straight line it comes alongside the ankle of the rear foot. Because your feet are in a straight line, you are able to turn round 180° and adopt the same position, but now in the other direction.

This position is of course dependent on the movement that Tori wishes to move to and so it is variable. In principle, it is also possible to shorten the distance between the feet. The forward knee is still always kept well bent.

In the on guard position, the upper body is kept upright (one speaks of an upright longitudinal axis). The shoulders are relaxed and pulled back slightly. The arms are held down loosely without being slack – an air of readiness should be exuded.

In this position, Tori can work up a good feeling in time of how to keep a good stable triangular stance. For this, the rear foot forms the base of the triangle with the forward hand forming the tip of it.

Seen from the front, as a result Tori is offering the minimum area of target to any attacker. When Uke and Tori are standing opposite each other, you can imagine two triangles opposing each other with their tips touching each other when, for example, Uke executes a *gyaku-hanmi katate dori* (see Page 275).

ai-hanmi and gyaku-hanmi

When starting a movement in Aikido, there are two positions *(hanmi)* in which Uke and Tori can stand facing each other:

- Diagonally *(ai-hanmi)*: Both lead with the same leg.

- Mirror-image *(gyaku-hanmi)*: Tori has his right leg forward and Uke his left leg or vice versa.

In the beginning in Aikido, Uke assumes his position from Tori's lead. Both sides are practiced – usually alternately.

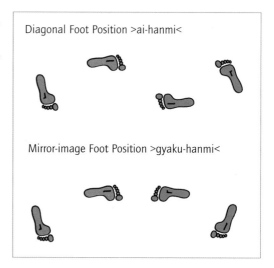

Diagonal Foot Position >ai-hanmi<

Mirror-image Foot Position >gyaku-hanmi<

2.2 Changing Foot on the Spot

The first basic exercise to be learned in foot movements is changing foot on the spot. From the on guard position, just mentioned, you pull your feet together. To do this, first of all the leading foot has to make a little room for the rear foot. Then the other foot is moved back.

In this exercise, note the following:

- The hips are not lifted up, but remain held low down throughout the whole movement i.e., the knees are well bent.

- Although the leg that was first of all the forward one is moved to the rear, the hips stay over the one spot. It is just the side that comes forward so that the whole body is not moved to and fro.

- The upper body remains upright and you look straight ahead.

- Arms and shoulders are relaxed. The shoulder and the arm on the side of the leading foot are also held forward.

- When practicing the changeover of feet, it is advisable to make a pause in order to firm up your stability. Advanced pupils should practice being able to changeover the feet as fast as possible.

In the changeover of the feet, not only do you change foot but also the other side of the body comes forward. In Aikido, one speaks of a left hip and a right hip stance. Not only the feet change, the hips change sides also.

2.3 irimi

One fundamental foot movement in Aikido is called *irimi* in Japanese. This is where a step (the rear leg comes forward) or gliding step (a sliding shuffle step) is made forward. The movement is characterized by the following points:

- Without pausing, Tori moves straight into an attack on Uke.

- As a result, Tori enters Uke's radius of action and could strike him with an *atemi* (a punch to stop or immobilize Uke).

- In order to imagine how this movement appears, run two pieces of paper past each other.

In the first example of the *irimi*, Uke attacks with a *jodan tsuki* (punch at Tori's face – see Page 281). Ideally, the distance is so large that Uke has to take another step in order to reach Tori). The feet are in the *gyaku-hanmi* stance.

At the moment that Uke starts his attack, Tori also moves – from his stable position – by already bringing his rear leg forward.

When Uke thinks he can strike Tori, Tori glides past Uke's punch and enters Uke's radius of action. Without stopping Uke's movement or pushing him aside, Tori takes control of Uke's punch with the diagonal hand.

Using this *irimi* movement, Tori now has a number of possibilities to apply other Aikido techniques before Uke can recover to attack again or get into a new position.

It is important in this movement that Tori's diagonal hand catches Uke's punch gently so that he doesn't signal to Uke what he is up to. In this way the punch is not blocked or changed in any way.

In the second example, we see the *irimi* action using a sword (see Chapter 2.10).

Uke attacks Tori with a *bokken* (training sword made of wood) using the *shomen uchi* action (straight sweep downwards at the head).

So that Uke can reach Tori, first of all he has to pull back the sword over his body axis and then take a gliding step forwards towards Tori to hit him.

During Uke's action, Tori moves in with a sliding shuffle step forwards. Simultaneously he brings his sword towards Uke's throat thus making Uke stop.

The following becomes clear in this example:

- The concept of irimi can be very direct.

- The forward movement must be far enough in order to actually stop Uke.

- Tori must be convinced in what he is doing and not be afraid.

- Tori and Uke move very much at the same time.

- Uke controls his attack actions in order to be in a position to react to Tori's movements

Again, the example also shows well that *irimi* is not just only a foot or body movement but also a mental exercise i.e., being able to go into a positive and controlled attack on Uke – without fear and with self-confidence. The saying by Morihei Ueshiba, the creator of Aikido, "Aikido is based on *irimi-atemi*" shows accordingly that Tori has the opportunity to be able to strike Uke effectively already in the first action.

2.4   tenkan

The opposite to the direct *irimi* movement is *tenkan*. In the *tenkan* movement, the leading foot is used to pivot the body round 180° to the rear. Tori's front foot is also further forward after the movement. The following points for the pivoting movement should be particularly noted:

*   The movement appears to be circular, but actually is straight i.e., just as in changing the foot on the spot the feet move in a straight line (see Chapter 2.2). The rear foot does not go round in a semicircle when turning.
*   The upper body remains straight and does not oscillate throughout the whole movement.
*   Beginners learn in Aikido to turn quicker and cleaner if they fix their eyes on a point straight away afterwards.
*   After turning round, it is advisable to hold for a second or two in order to regain stability. As an advanced pupil, one tries to execute the turn as quickly as possible and continually sharpen up the movement.

An example of the movement is with Uke – in a mirror-image stance *(gyaku-hanmi)* – grabbing hold of Tori's wrist *(katate dori* – see Page 275). Uke's and Tori's feet are all on a line with each other.

Uke now serves as a non-resisting partner for Tori's movements i.e., he acts neutrally and neither pulls nor pushes. Tori begins with a sliding shuffle step forwards just slightly past Uke. In the movement, he brings his arm onto his body without Uke pulling or pushing as he grips him.

Tori bends his gripped hand away so that the fingers point away from Uke. Tori's and Uke's forces are now not opposing each other, but rather are flowing in the same direction.

Because Uke's grip leads along Tori's longitudinal axis and while this also forms the pivot point of the whole movement, Tori can now turn round backwards 180°, pivoting on his leading foot.

After the turn, Tori ends up in the basic on guard position in a firm stance.

This exercise is called *tenkan-ho* (*'ho'* = exercise, studying a principle, see Chapter 6).

Here we show the details of the hand position just prior to the turn backwards. Tori's thumb and Uke's arm lie in a line.

When the wrist is grabbed hold of, Tori and Uke slowly try to imagine a picture that a triangle is formed where both of their hands meet at the tip of it.

In the *tenkan* movement – with the grip shown earlier particularly in mind – it is not just only to do with the turning action, because Tori could practice this alone. Rather it is also about finding a joint point of contact. By using a grip this is relatively simple, because, first of all Uke and Tori are not moving. Later on, Uke can attack with a step and Tori tries to find the same contact point with more dynamic aim. This is the basic premise for executing rapid and effective movements. Here, the first moment of contact is of particular importance – the Japanese word for this is *'de-ai'*.

2.5   tai-sabaki

Irimi and *tenkan* constitute the main elements of a basic foot movement in Aikido called *'tai-sabaki'* meaning literally "moving the body *('tai')*". Generally, in Aikido this is taken to mean an action consisting of *'irimi'* – taking a step forwards – and *'tenkan'* – turning round backwards. In other words – one step, one turn. It is not necessary in the turn to have to go through exactly 180°.

A specific feeling for the movement belongs in the sequence of these movements. On the one hand, the tension created in the *'irimi'* element of the technique is dissolved in the *'tenkan'* element. In ideal cases, this happens when the maximum tension is reached by Tori moving in directly. A central part of the exercise *'tai-sabaki'* – and Aikido itself – is found by experiencing when and where the point of highest tension exists.

On the other hand, *'tai-sabaki'* indicates that the initial, opposing forces meet and these are developed further from this point – usually led by Tori.

The sequence of movements in the *'tai-sabaki'* can be practiced by the *Aikido-ka* alone. In this, the following points are important:

• The feet move along a line i.e., not in a semi-circle. This is the only way to ensure rapid and effective movements later on.

• The upper body remains straight and does not oscillate.

• The hips are kept as low as possible at the same height and the knees are bent.

• After the turn, a positive, forward direction of movement is reassumed.

Hands and shoulders remain loose and relaxed, hanging down over the feet. The forward hand is the one on the side of the leading foot.

As in previous exercises, it is advisable to pause for a second or two after the movement in order to regain your stability.

Relative to Uke, *tai-sabaki* can be performed on the forward side *('omote')* of Uke or on his rear side *('ura')*.

First of all the movement is carried out on Uke's rear side (after the movement, Tori is standing behind Uke). Uke attacks with a *chudan tsuki* (punch at the stomach – see Page 282). The gap between them is so large that Uke has to take another step to reach Tori.

At the moment that Uke begins to move forward, Tori also starts to move.

When Uke thinks he can strike Tori, Tori slides past the punch *('irimi')*. Thus Tori's outer hand can control Uke's punch without having to push him outwards to do so.

In the ideal case, Tori moves close enough past Uke's punch to graze past Tori's clothing. In this moment of maximum tension, Tori turns round backwards pivoting on his leading foot and then stands behind Uke's back in a firm stance. Both are now looking in the same direction.

It is important in this movement that Tori should have the possibility before the movement to strike Uke himself with an *'atemi'* – i.e., the turn should not be done too early.

Alternatively – in other words – because Tori has the possibility of striking Uke at the initial moment, and thereby theoretically ending Uke's attack, he refrains from doing this and turns himself round backwards.

It will be plain to see, that Aikido means to act from a point of strength – this is not to be confused in any way with dodging and feinting movements, running away or passiveness!

Now we turn to the *'tai-sabaki'* executed on Uke's forward side. Uke attacks with a *gyaku-hanmi katate dori* (see Page 275). In order to get hold of Tori's wrist he has to take a further step forwards – the starting position is from *ai-hanmi*.

At the moment that Uke begins to move forwards, Tori starts to move with his rear leg. Now Tori is clearly going to one side of the line that Uke and Tori were first standing along.

Tori's rear hand comes forward with the movement of the foot and controls the distance without influencing the flow of movement.

At the moment when Uke grabs hold of Tori' wrist, Tori turns round pivoting on his forward foot and brakes Uke's forward impetus.

Uke remains the attacker and corrects his position with Tori by readjusting it (see Chapter 8.1).

At the end of the movement, Tori is standing at Uke's forward side and is able to follow up with various Aikido techniques. Uke's and Tori's feet are now in a diagonally opposed position, because Tori has changed foot as he turned.

In this movement, Tori doesn't pull with his hand at all.

2.6   tai no henka

Like *'tai-sabaki'*, this foot movement constitutes one of the main elements of many Aikido techniques and alongside *irimi* and *tenkan* provides us with the third basic movement sequence. In *tai no henka*, the direction of movement is swung through 180° without the leg stance changing – only the feet and the hips are turned. As in *tenkan*, the upper body is kept upright and does not oscillate or become bent forward.

After the movement, Tori and Uke should get the idea in their minds of a triangle formed with the tip at the point where Uke is gripped (see Page 44).

In the following sequence of movements, as before in the *tenkan* action, Uke takes hold of Tori's wrist in a *gyaku-hanmi katate dori* grip. The feet are positioned in a mirror-image stance and all four feet are placed in a line.

As in the *tenkan* action, Tori begins by taking a sliding shuffle step forwards and in so doing brings his arm to his body without pulling or pushing. At the same, Tori bends his wrist so that the fingers are pointing away from Uke (see detailed photo on Page 44).

Tori and Uke are now applying their force in the same direction again.

Unlike in the *tenkan*, Tori now does not turn round backwards, but glides further behind Uke with his front foot leading and turns his hips and feet through 180°.

Uke and Tori are looking in the same direction. Both have the same foot forward.

A good example of the use of tai no henka can be seen in its application in the technique *shiho nage* (see Chapter 5.9). As soon as Tori has avoided Uke's attack by using a *tai-sabaki* action (see Chapter 2.5}, he grabs hold of both of Uke's hands. Tori and Uke are now standing diagonally opposed to each other.

Tori now takes a step forwards *(irimi)*.

Then Tori changes the direction of his movement by turning his hips through 180° *(tai no henka)*. So that Tori can do this he brings his arm up slightly. It is important in this action not to pull the arms outwards. Tori's arms remain permanently on his longitudinal axis and his elbows remain pointing downwards and not rotated outwards.

2.7 Foot Movements - 90° Angles

Besides the movements described already, 90° changes of direction also play an important role in basic foot movements in Aikido. Yet again, these movements illustrate that the thought basis in Aikido lies in actions taken positively against an attacker.

First of all we cover a 90° movement by Tori in the direction of Uke's front side *(omote)*. Uke attacks with a *kata dori* (gripping the jacket at shoulder height – see Page 275). The distance between Tori and Uke is so large so that Uke has to take a further step to reach Tori's shoulder.

At the moment Uke starts his attack, Tori also begins to move. He takes one step forwards *(irimi)*. The rear hand controls the distance to Uke for this.

At the moment when Uke starts taking hold of Tori's jacket, Tori changes his direction of movement turning 90° outwards. To do this he places his rear foot and leg at a 90° angle relative to his starting position.

Tori's hand, that was controlling the distance to Uke, moves onto Uke's elbow and brings it outwards at a 90° angle.

Because of the movement on his elbow and the potential danger of being struck by Tori's other hand, Uke goes with the outwards direction of movement and rolls over forwards.

This is at the same time a good example that the more demanding Aikido techniques rely on learning and intelligent actions being applied by Uke (see Chapter 8). For example, if he were simply to relax his arm in this exercise then he would not be able to react adequately. From this point of view, this movement is also not a pure basic movement. This is because Uke has to have learned a particular movement pattern, in order to have a meaningful answer to Tori's movements. Another conclusion is that, in Aikido, Uke's and Tori's progress is mutually conditional (see Chapter 7).

For clarity here are the foot movements once again – without Uke.

We now cover the 90° movement on Uke's rear side *(ura)*. The *kata dori* attack is used again. Uke takes a further step in order to reach Tori's shoulder.

Differently to the first movement, Tori begins by taking a sliding shuffle step forwards and outwards.

At the moment when Uke reaches Tori's shoulder, Tori changes the direction of his movement by turning through a 90° angle. To do this he places his rear foot at an angle of 90° to his starting position. At the same time, Tori's rear hand controls Uke's forward shoulder.

Uke is brought off-balance by Tori's movements. His hand functions now as a "hand-off" prop against Tori, and Uke rolls over forwards.

For clarity here are the foot movements once again – without Uke.

2.8   tsugi ashi

Besides the basic foot movements described already, at the beginning of an Aikido technique you will often find gliding steps being taken *(tsugi ashi)*. These have the purpose of changing/closing the gap between Tori and Uke or initiating the technique.

A gliding (sliding shuffle) step is done by sliding the leading foot forwards while the rear foot presses forwards – vice versa if done in the other direction. During a technique, gliding steps are also used to change the distance between Tori and Uke.

In the following example of the movement Uke attacks using a *mae geri* (kick at the stomach – see Page 283).

By taking a gliding step forwards, Tori can shorten the gap to Uke so that he, for example, can then glide past Uke's feet as in *irimi*.

In this, Tori's movement is only just a little to the outside.

He glides past Uke's feet at the moment that Uke believes he can strike Tori.

At the moment when Uke thinks he can reach Tori, Tori can also take a gliding step backwards in order to give more distance between them.

For this, up to the moment that Uke actually kicks out, the distance must be such that Uke can still reach Tori. If Tori went back too early, Uke would follow him firstly and then attack him. In the example shown here, Tori has increased the gap at the last moment before Uke attacks.

2.9   shikko

Being able to move about on the knees is also a part of the basic foot techniques. Since Aikido stems from Japan, this form of exercise has, on the one hand an historical background and on the other hand it gives one the opportunity to establish a feeling for holding the hips firmly or to develop a feeling of a stable base (see Chapter 6.1). The leg muscles are also trained and the *Aikido-ka* can easily feel whether he is keeping his upper body upright.

Basically, the following points are of note:

- The toes are propped up.
- The upper body is kept straight.
- The bottom is resting as far as possible on the heels.
- The heels are kept together as far as possible.
- At least one knee is always touching the mat.
- When turning, the knees must come together to form a pivot axis.
- If one of the knees is lifted up for the movement, the angle between the thigh and the lower leg must be less than 90°.

First of all the sequence of movements without Uke – this can be practiced by the beginner easily on his own.

The first principle (*ikkyo* – see Chapter 5.1) is demonstrated in the following example of the movements. As in all the techniques, it can be executed in front of (*omote*) or behind (*ura*) Uke.

shomen uchi ikkyo omote waza

First of all, the *omote* version: The starting position is such that Uke has to move forwards to reach Tori.

To do this, Uke attacks using a *shomen uchi* (straight strike downwards at the head – see Page 279). He takes his rear hand up over his head and places the rear knee up forwards. At the same time, Tori places his forward knee forwards to one side and prepares himself to get out of the line of Uke's attack.

Uke glides further forward and strikes at Tori's head. Tori places his forward knee down on the mat and lifts his rear knee up forwards *(shikko)*. At the same time, he lifts his forward arm to ward off Uke's strike. He does not attack, but glides his hand up along Uke's lower arm. Tori's rear arm grabs hold of Uke's elbow.

With the forward movement of his rear knee, Uke sweeps his front ankle away and lands on his lower arm.

Then Tori brings his arms down in front of his own longitudinal axis and finishes the movement this way. In the downward movement, Tori – using his diagonal hand – grabs hold of Uke's wrist (above the palm of the hand). With this key position, he can control Uke.

Tori places his forward knee now down forwards and his rear knee outwards and forwards. He now holds Uke's shoulder.

Tori then places his knee forwards and brings Uke's shoulder down on the mat. Uke relaxes his shoulder – he doesn't lie down of his own accord, but follows Tori's movement.

The final position of ikkyo: Tori's inner knee is against Uke's shoulder and the outer knee is against his wrist. The bottom is resting on his heels, the toes are propped up and the back is held straight. Uke's arm is being held firmly but not pressed down on the mat.

shomen uchi ikkyo ura waza

Now the *ura* movement: Uke attacks again as in omote waza. However, Tori now starts by placing his rear knee forwards and outwards.

The gap between them is such that Uke has to move one step forwards to reach Tori.

As in the *omote*, Tori's diagonal arm is checking Uke's attack without gripping. The other hand grips Uke's elbow.

Tori now brings his knees forward together to get into a pivot position and turns round 180° to the rear. In this movement, he brings his hands downwards and in front of his longitudinal axis while he brings first of all Uke's shoulders on to the ground. In this downwards movement, Tori is gripping Uke's wrist just above the palm of the hand using the diagonal hand.

Uke submits, relaxing under the pressure and lets his shoulder go loose.

After turning, Tori spreads his knees out again and controls Uke. Tori's inner knee is pushed into the hollow of Uke's shoulder and the outer knee is placed on the wrist. The bottom is resting on his heels with the toes propped up and his back is held straight. Uke's arm is firmly held but not pressed down onto the mat (see above).

In these movements, the following points are important:

- In *omote*, you should gradually work up to using a gliding forwards movement. The knees are not placed down hard, rather the rear knee comes forward again immediately.

- The direction of movement in *omote* is characterized by leaving Uke's attacking line to the outside, returning into his attacking line in order to put Uke off-balance and then leaving the attacking line once more in order to get Uke down onto his stomach.

- In *ura*, the turning motion is done deliberately and firmly. Gradually, Tori should try to speed up the turn.

- During the turning motion the knees must be together.

2.10 Foot Positions for Sword Exercises

There are a lot of similarities between the exercises with the sword *(bokken)* and techniques in Aikido. Inter alia, this has a lot to do with the way the feet are moved and what positions the *Aikido-ka* adopts.

seigan kamae

The feet are behind each other in a line. The leading foot is pointing directly forwards while the rear foot is in the direction of movement. Pulling the leading foot back to the rear one, the heel touches the ankle.

Turning now at right angles, the feet are closed and are together alongside each other. Turning yet further, you are in the same position as before but now round 180°. This means that these foot positions allow you to turn round 180° easily – in Aikido, a very important aspect.

mu kamae

This position – often used in *kenjutsu* – emphasizes particularly the low stance that

allows you to be able to move immediately forward. In this position the feet are further apart than in the *seigan kamae*, but still behind each other in a line. The leading foot is turned outwards slightly – the knee and the foot are aligned.

The forward knee is well bent and the rear leg is held firmly. The bottom is tensed so that you don't get a hollow back.

waki kamae

The low stance is also particularly important in this position. The sword is held to the rear along the side of the body so that it is not seen from the front. The leading foot is placed slightly outwards and the knees are well bent.

All the foot positions shown in this chapter can also be practiced by the *Aikido-ka* easily alone. The following points should be noted:

- Start off slowly and give yourself time. The movements look simple – but this is what makes them difficult. It is particularly important to pause a second or two after each movement in order to check your stability and be able to correct it.

- Develop a feeling for the straight movements. Sometimes, Aikido movements are compared to dancing steps. The movements should, however, not always get too rounded – quite the opposite. In the long run, only straight movements can achieve rapid actions and motions. It is therefore important to emphasize that the foot positions in Aikido are executed in straight-line movements and not in semi-circular ones.

- In all exercises, the upper body remains upright and does not oscillate.

- Gradually the turning motions must be done cleaner thus increasing the speed of their execution.

- Arms and hands remain relaxed and are not held slack but, rather indicate a certain small amount of tension.

- The shoulders are loose and slightly pulled back.

- The eyes are kept looking forwards. When turning, a focus point should be fixed on as quickly as possible.

"All art is but imitation of nature."

Lucius Seneca

3 Hand Movements

- How do you move your hands in Aikido?
- Why does Uke grip Tori's wrist?
- How does Tori react to punches and kicks?

In Aikido, you practice very different forms of attack. This gives you a broad spectrum of movement possibilities that you can learn. A compilation of all the forms of attack used in Aikido is in Chapter 8.3.

Attacks that involve gripping allow you to learn the movements slowly and also allow you to gain sensitivity for the quality of the movement performed. The *Aikido-ka* needs this in order, for example, to be able to deal with punches or kicks effectively.

In principle, when using grips the following is to be noted:

- Generally, the forward leg is the one that is on the same side as the forward arm.
- The grip is firm but relaxed with the shoulders remaining loose.
- The little finger is used to grip hard with the ring finger not gripping quite so much etc. The thumb exerts the same pressure as all the other 4 fingers on the hand together.
- The palm of Uke's hand is in full contact with Tori's wrist.
- If the grip is not used, the arm remains relaxed without becoming slack. The elbow remains flexible.
- Uke does not push forward (i.e., to push Tori out of the way – this does not usually constitute an attack).
- In the movements covered below, Tori uses his hand like a sword with the side of the hand acting as the edge *(te-gatana)*.

3.1 Hand Movements from an ai-hanmi katate dori

Ai-hanmi katate dori is where the diagonal hand grips Tori's wrist. This grip must be seen more as an interesting learning aid and less as an attack, because with his grip at the angle that Uke is standing in relation to Tori, he cannot exercise control.

Tori is able to give his hand forward so that his thumb is either uppermost or is underneath when his arm is twisted round. There are five different options to deal with Uke's grip.

First Option

Tori's thumb is uppermost.

Tori grasps hold of Uke's wrist and then uses his thumb to open Uke's guard (to the right when gripping the right arm and vice versa).

He takes care that his elbow is not rotated outwards. Tori could now strike Uke with his free hand *(atemi)*. At the same time, he prevents Uke reaching him.

Examples of techniques that can be used to follow on are:
shiho nage omote, ude kime nage omote, koshi nage

Second Option

Tori's thumb is uppermost.

Tori brings his wrist back and up a little without pulling.

He then moves the edge of his hand (on the side of his little finger) round Uke's wrist. As in the first option, Tori takes care that he doesn't rotate his elbow outwards in this movement.

Tori's hand then comes onto the other side of Uke's wrist. If Tori continued with his movement, Uke's grip would be broken. Because Uke remains relaxed, he can maintain his grip.

One technique that can be used to follow on is, for example, *kote gaeshi*.

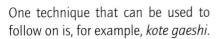

Third Option

Tori's thumb is uppermost.

Tori takes a step past Uke *(irimi)* and at the same time turns his palm over upwards.

Tori turns his hips round 180° *(tai no henka)*. Uke's grip begins to break.

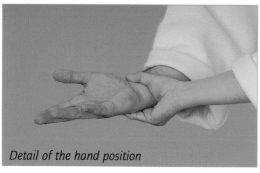

Detail of the hand position

Examples of techniques that can be used to follow on are:
kote gaeshi, uchi kaiten nage, uchi kaiten sankyo.

Fourth Option

Tori's thumb is uppermost.

Tori takes a step past Uke and at the same time turns his palm over downwards.

Different to the previous movement, Tori's thumb is pointing towards Uke. Thus, first of all, Uke can keep hold of it. Tori can now reach Uke with his free hand *(atemi)*; in other words, Uke's guard is now open.

Examples of techniques that can be used to follow on are:
uchi kaiten nage, uchi kaiten sankyo.

Fifth Option

Tori's thumb is now underneath as his arm is twisted round.

Tori now brings his hand in a semi-circular motion outwards and upwards in front of his longitudinal axis in the direction of Uke's finger.

In this, Tori's arm is neither stretched out nor bent in but has a slightly rounded form (te-gatana).

Examples of techniques that can be used to follow on are:
ikkyo, nikkyo, irimi nage.

3.2   Hand Movements from a gyaku-hanmi katate dori

Gyaku-hanmi katate dori is where Tori's opposite wrist (mirror-image) is being gripped. In the angle that he is standing in relation to Tori, this grip makes it possible for Uke to keep control.

As in the *ai-hanmi katate dori*, Tori is able to give his hand forward so that his thumb is either uppermost or is underneath when his arm is twisted round. There are five different options to deal with Uke's grip.

First Option

Tori's thumb is uppermost.

Tori brings his hand downwards and outwards in a semi-circular motion and then brings the edge of his hand back up in the direction of Uke's head.

Uke's grip is relaxed so that he can maintain it further.

At the end of the movement , Tori's hand is in front of his longitudinal axis. As in the previous option his arm is neither fully stretched out nor bent in.

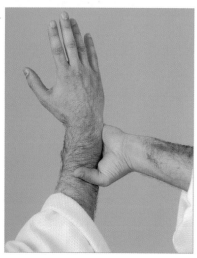

One technique that can be used to follow on is, for example, *soto kaiten nage.*

Detail of the hand position

Second Option

Tori's thumb is uppermost.

Tori bends his wrist so that his fingers are pointing towards him. At the same time he takes a sliding shuffle step forwards thus bringing his body towards his arm.

From above, the free hand controls Uke's lower arm and wrist as Tori grasps it.

Then Tori turns his hips through 180° without changing the position of his feet (see *tai no henka* in Chapter 2.6)

Examples of techniques that can be used to follow on are:
irimi nage, shiho nage, ude kime nage

Third Option

Tori's thumb is uppermost.

Tori turns the palm of his hand over to face downwards and the thumb now is pointing towards him.

Taking a sliding shuffle step forwards, he turns his elbow to point forwards. His gripped wrist forms the pivot axis for his elbow and he doesn't pull at Uke's grip.

Tori's free hand moves downwards between Uke's grip and Tori's lower arm thus finally breaking Uke's grip.

Throughout this movement, Tori watches out to keep at distance from Uke. At the end of the movement his own arm is not close to his body.

Examples of techniques that can be used to follow on are:
kote gaeshi, kokyu nage.

Fourth Option

Tori's thumb is uppermost.

Tori takes a gliding shuffle step forwards and brings his gripped hand upwards and inwards in a semi-circle – he can now see the palm of his own hand.

The free hand now crosses upwards between Uke's lower arm and Tori's lower arm thus breaking Uke's grip.

Examples of techniques that can be used to follow on are:
irimi nage, soto kaiten nage

Detail of the hand positions (turned 180°)

Fifth Option

Tori's thumb is underneath.

Tori brings the edge of his hand slightly upwards and then outwards round Uke's wrist

This movement is easier if Tori changes the position of his feet. During the movement, Tori keeps his hands always in front of his longitudinal axis.

At the end of the downwards movement he can grip hold of Uke's wrist himself thus controlling Uke's elbow.

Examples of techniques that can be used to follow on are:
shiho nage, ude kime nage.

3.3 Grips Against the Sword

How to react to both of the attacks – *ai-hanmi katate dori* and *gyaku-hanmi katate dori* – or how Tori's hand movements already covered, can be shown more clearly by looking at work using the sword.

For example, Uke's grip in the *ai-hanmi katate dori* prevents Tori from drawing his sword.

Uke positions himself in such a way that in the *gyaku-hanmi katate dori*, Tori cannot strike him with the hilt of the sword.

In other words, Tori and Uke are standing facing each other in the following position: Uke's grip is directed at Tori's longitudinal axis, while Tori's hand or sword is directed past Uke. Both are not standing directly opposite each other.

Uke

Tori

When the first movement in the ai-hanmi katate dori is upwards (see Page 74) this equates to the sword being drawn upwards out of its sheath.

Uke takes a step forward and grasps hold of Tori's wrist with his diagonal hand. However, Tori is already in the process of drawing his sword upwards out of its sheath.

Alternatively, Tori can control Uke by applying a pinning action on the wrist using the hilt of the sword (*nikkyo ura* – see Chapter 5.2) after having been grasped diagonally by him. Tori can now draw his sword completely and thus control Uke.

Detail of position of sword and hands

3.4   Hand Movements Against Punches and Kicks

By practicing the techniques against attacks where a grip is involved you also gain confidence in being able to deal with punches and kicks. At the beginning of your study of Aikido this is not so much to do with realistic usage, but rather more to do with being able to convincingly control the punches and kicks (for the difference between techniques and application see Chapter 7.3).

This controlling action will give Tori self-confidence in dealing with attacks and in due course allow him to learn to use softer and smoother movements – as can be seen clearly in the examples that follow (using the hand movements already covered so far).

Uke and Tori are standing in a diagonally opposed position opposite each other.

Uke uses a *chudan tsuki* strike (straight punch at the stomach). At the point of contact of the punch, the position of the feet is as in *ai-hanmi*, since Tori as well as Uke take a step forward in this movement.

With the forward stepping motion, Tori stops Uke by using the edge of his hand on Uke's leading shoulder and without pushing it back.

Tori's arm has to be sufficiently tensed and must not give even with a strong attack. However, the arm is simultaneously not fully stretched out.

Tori's stance must be down low and stable in order to effectively stop Uke. The upper body remains upright.

If the movement is correctly executed, Uke cannot reach Tori.

The edge of the hand is against Uke's shoulder

Uke attacks with a *mae geri* (kick at the stomach). Tori is able to glide back slightly *(tsugi ashi)* in order to make the gap bigger for Uke (see Chapter 2.8).

His forward hand comes down in a diagonal cutting movement and controls Uke's kick. The kick is deflected slightly outwards.

Tori's hand movement is sustained but always in front of his longitudinal axis.

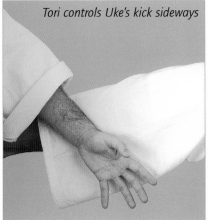

Tori controls Uke's kick sideways

Uke attacks with a *chudan tsuki*.

Tori takes a step past Uke's punch *(irimi)* – and, just at the moment when the highest tension had been reached i.e., just as Uke thinks he can strike Tori.

His outer hand controls Uke's elbow. His forward hand is moved in a cutting motion inwards, thus maintaining the gap to Uke.

To control the gap means that when Tori glides further forward or gets too close to Uke, Tori can strike Uke's head.

Uke attacks using a *jodan tsuki* (punch to the head – see Page 281). At the moment of the strike, the position of the feet is in a diagonal stance *(ai-hanmi)*.

Tori glides back to increase the gap for Uke and controls Uke's arm or punch with his forward diagonal hand.

At the same time he doesn't sweep Uke's arm outwards away, but takes up the movement and keeps his hand in front of his longitudinal axis.

While doing so, the arm must be sufficiently tensed in order to be able to take up Uke's punch. Tori adopts a relatively low stance.

Uke attacks using a chudan tsuki.

Tori glides forward and turns his hips *(tai no henka)*.

At the same time, by rotating his shoulders, he brings the edge of his hand outwards.
Of course, the elbows also rotate with this movement, but are not lifted up.

Contact happens just at the moment that Uke thinks he can hit Tori.

In this way, the inner arm controls Uke's punch. Tori needs to adopt a stable position in order to withstand the blow of the contact. With continued practice, Tori tries more and more to take up Uke's position at the moment of contact.

Taking a step forwards, Uke attacks with a *chudan tsuki*. Tori glides forward *(tsugi ashi)*, controlling Uke's punch with his outer hand at the same time.

Tori's brings his free hand downwards and controls Uke's punch additionally with it.

In this movement, Tori has three ways of not being hit by the punch: a) The gliding step forwards and outwards, b) By having the outer hand on the elbow and c) The use of the inner hand as it is brought downwards. Each part of this should suffice in itself to avoid Uke's punch.

Detail of hand positions

89

Taking a step forwards, Uke attacks using a *jodan tsuki* punch. Tori takes a gliding shuffle step forwards.

Tori controls the punch without deflecting it out sideways.

The rear hand is brought up and is used additionally to control Uke's attack. Tori's upper body remains upright and his stance is low and stable.

Both arms are sufficiently tensed in order to control Uke's punch.

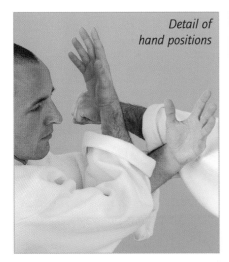

Detail of
hand positions

Christian Tissier and Martina Dorka – kote gaeshi

"Education is an admirable thing, but it is well to remember from time to time that nothing that is worth knowing can be taught."

Oscar Wilde

4 Working up Techniques

- How do you go about working up techniques in Aikido?

- How do you gain self-confidence and self-assurance?

- How can Tori use what he has worked up in Aikido?

The basic techniques in Aikido do not function in a realistic attack. Why do we learn them then?

By asking this question you arrive at a paradox that is essential to understand when learning Aikido as a martial art. The answer to this apparent contradiction lies in the realization that the basic techniques that are there, are the ones made by the person learning when practicing them himself, and are not for use in action against your exercise partner or against an attacker.

This means that the basic techniques make it possible for the *Aikido-ka* to develop the following qualities:

- The *Aikido-ka* can grasp the logical sequence of the techniques i.e., he understands the laid down foot and hand movements and can internalize them.

- He can work up a low and safe stance i.e., the specific-to-Aikido positions are being practiced and a specific-to-Aikido muscular system is being built up.

- The use of the arms and the hands is learned i.e., practicing surety in stopping and controlling punches and exercising competence in executing the grips oneself.

- On top of these is learning the correct timing in a situation. This doesn't mean not only being in the right place at the right time, but, with experience, also being able to judge correctly one's own potential and that of the opponent.

- Finally, by practicing the basic techniques, the underlying principles of all techniques are recognized, understood and internalized (see Chapter 6).

Therefore, the purpose of the basic techniques is to allow the *Aikido-ka* to develop these five qualities and continue to improve them, because they form the roots of Aikido as a form of movement skill. In this, one works mainly on oneself and far less against an exercise partner. The latter represents rather more the necessary and appropriate obstacle in the way of the person exercising;

- so that a good sequence of movements in a technique can be learned, an exercise partner is required as a corrective.

- because one can only speak of a stable stance when one is present.

- because the same applies to a sure grip and stopping punches. This kind of surety can only be learned in relation to Uke's attacks.

- An excellent example of the idea of training together with an exercise partner can be seen in having good timing – after all, without a partner, the *Aikido-ka* cannot even begin to realize what his timing is.

The efforts expended on practicing the basic techniques can also be called 'working up' the techniques. In other words: By reciprocal practice together or against each other, Tori and Uke can work up the points above.

The emphasis here is laid on constructive mutual cooperation. When Uke attacks, he gives Tori the opportunity to learn by it and vice versa. For this to be successful, Tori has to rely on Uke presenting himself as a sensible and interesting attacker, because he can only make progress in this way.

The working up process is the same for anyone practicing. Depending on his physical ability, as the only difficulty in attacking Tori, Uke must vary his strength. People with less strength have to exert the same effort as those who are stronger – of course all relative to the less strength they possess. In normal training, however, it is quite possible that a considerably stronger *Aikido-ka* will block a weaker one. In the light of the concept being developed here, this would appear to be of little value. In contrast, the aim of working up is to be increasingly less reliant on physical strength. The principles of Aikido should be used more effectively instead.

When the points referred to above have been internalized after many years of practicing, only then can the basic techniques be modified so that they can function without cooperative help from Uke. This is then the turning point where the lessons learned can now be put into realistically functioning practice.

It is important to understand the difference between learning the basic techniques, with the relative working up process, and the area of application of these experiences and abilities, resulting from the working up sessions themselves.

If situations occur in training for Aikido, where the person exercising ascertains that their movements do not function when Uke acts in a particular way, then there are three possible reasons for this: a) Tori is not advanced sufficiently enough in his working up process, b) Tori employs techniques against Uke that are not meant to be used against Uke- namely, the Aikido basic techniques, or c) Uke has not understood his constructive role as an attacker and blocks the movement in an inappropriate manner.

It has already been mentioned often (see Chapter 1), that the Aikido techniques also represent a method of so-called mental work. Relating to the working up process, this means that the mental condition is also affected by the way in which the physical work up is done. From this point of view, it is important that the working up process leads to an 'exchange' or form of 'communication'.

In the following, we cover a few examples to explain the working up process further.

4.1   katate ryote dori

ikkyo omote waza

Uke attacks using a *katate ryote dori* (grasping one of Tori's arms in both hands – see Page 276). To a certain degree, this form of attack allows Tori to learn the use of arms and hands, because Uke poses a considerable difficulty for Tori this way.

Tori takes a gliding step forwards and outwards, but without pushing or pulling. As he does this, he brings his elbow forward and bends both of his knees down deeply. In this movement Uke's grip forms the pivot axis for Tori's elbow. Uke holds on well but with his arms and shoulders relaxed.

Tori now pivots on his leading foot *(tenkan)* and at the same time brings his hand up in front of his longitudinal axis. Uke carries on holding his grip firmly but relaxed and tries not to block the movement, but does not lead the way. In so doing he acts in an appropriate manner and permits Tori to do his work up.

Tori now brings his arm slightly downwards and forwards while at the same time turning his thumb to underneath. Uke follows this movement by taking a step forwards.

The following photos are now shown turned at right angles

Tori now changes over feet on the spot (see Chapter 2.2). Tori and Uke bend their knees down as far as possible. The rear knee is tensed outwards. Both can adopt a stable stance this way. Tori's and Uke's upper bodies are upright and their shoulders are in line with their feet (i.e., they are not standing front on to each other).

Tori's free hand controls the distance to Uke *(atemi)*.

Tori now grasps the back of Uke's hand and brings his hand, still holding Uke's hand, in a semi-circle upwards. The hand being gripped comes directly up to Uke's elbow at the same time. Uke relaxes his arm but maintains a stable position.

Tori takes a step forward and at the same time brings his arm down – he finishes this movement and can begin to control Uke.

Tori can change to all the other holding positions (see Chapter 5) from this key move.

Now Tori takes a further step forwards and outwards and at the same time, using his grip on the arm, he controls Uke's shoulder and brings it down on to the ground.

To take final control over Uke, Tori kneels down. The toes are propped up, the inner knee is in the armpit of Uke's shoulder and the outer one is beside Uke's wrist. The angle between the arm and Uke's body is just over 90°.

irimi nage

Uke and Tori are so far apart that Uke has to take a further step to close with Tori. As Uke moves forward (e.g., in order to grasp Tori's shoulders), Tori lifts his arm in the direction of Uke's face.

Uke tries to grasp hold of Tori's arm as this will provide an obstacle to him. Before Uke can really get hold, Tori twists his arm so that he is looking at the palm of his hand.

At the same time Tori takes a gliding step forwards and turns round 180° backwards on his leading foot *(tenkan)*.

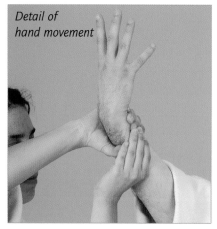

Detail of hand movement

This photo shows the same situation from the other angle (180°)

Uke takes a step forwards in order to bring Tori's arm down and control it with both hands.

Tori follows Uke's movement without pulling. At the same time, he brings his body against his arm and takes a step behind Uke before he manages to get into a stable position.

This photo shows the same situation from the other angle (180°)

Uke regains his balance by using his rear foot as a counter balance and turning backwards.

Tori is now controlling Uke's throat or neck area using his free hand and begins to turn round backwards. At the same time, he brings his arm (that is being gripped) downwards and follows the movement of his feet.

This brings Uke off-balance again. Uke stretches his rear leg out and follows the movement with his front foot. The inner hand touches the floor and the rear foot serves as a counter balance. Uke's grip is thus broken.

Tori turns his hips further *(tai no henka)*. Uke follows this movement.

Tori brings Uke's head onto his shoulder with one hand. The other arm is along the side of Uke's head with the thumb pointing downwards.

Tori now takes a gliding step forwards with his leading foot and brings his arm down. In this way, Uke is brought off-balance and thrown.

Uke drops down onto his inner knee on the mat and rolls over backwards.

The same situation seen from the other side (180°).

4.2   kata dori men uchi

kote gaeshi

Uke grasps hold of Tori's jacket at shoulder height with one of his hands and, using his diagonal hand, executes a strike downwards at Tori's head. Their foot positions are in the mirror-image stance (see Chapter 2.1).

Tori lifts his forward hand and controls Uke's strike by making it glide up past his lower arm. For this, Tori's arm must be sufficiently tensed in order to be able to stop Uke's strike.

At the same time, Tori takes a gliding step forwards and outwards and starts to turn round backwards.

Then he brings his leading foot to the rear and round 90° outwards. Uke follows this movement by controlling Tori's hand.

In this movement, Tori and Uke use their knees firmly by tensing them outwards. The upper bodies are held upright. Uke is still holding onto Tori's jacket. Both are controlling each other using their hands or their wrists.

Tori now grasps hold of Uke's wrist and the ball of his thumb using his upper hand (see Page 192). His little finger is on Uke's pulse.

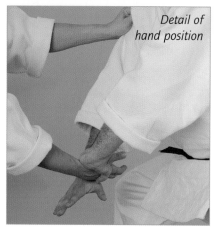

Detail of hand position

Tori now begins to turn his gripped wrist and at the same time bend Uke's wrist away. The wrist forms the pivot axis point. The motion is not carried out upwards but is kept at knee height.

In addition, Tori places his free hand on Uke's wrist and speeds the movement up. Uke rolls over backwards or falls forward over the pivot axis of his wrist.

Tori keeps hold of his grip on Uke's wrist. His other hand glides along Uke's lower arm to reach his elbow.

The thumb is pointing at Tori with this motion.

Tori now begins to move round Uke's head. The axis between Uke's hand and head forms the pivot axis for Tori's movement.

Tori rotates Uke's elbow around this axis (i.e., it is not pulled round). This movement turns Uke onto his stomach.

The same position seen from the other side (90°).

Tori kneels down so that Uke's shoulder is between his knees. He places Uke's arm into the bend of his elbow and grasps his opposite shoulder with his hand. The other hand bends Uke's arm and pulls it towards Tori's upper body.

Tori turns his hips in the direction of Uke's head and this applies a lever hold on his shoulder.

nikkyo ura waza

Uke grasps hold of Tori's jacket at shoulder height with one of his hands and, using his free hand, executes a strike downwards at Tori's head. Their foot positions are in the mirror-image stance.

Tori controls Uke's strike with his forward arm. His arm has to be well tensed so that he is not hit by Uke's strike. At the same time Tori takes a gliding step forwards and outwards and turns round 180° backwards pivoting on his leading foot.

Uke follows Tori's movement by taking a step forwards. Tori brings his feet together moving to the rear and turns outwards at right angles to his starting position. His free hand is controlling the gap between him and Uke.

Tori's hand now grasps hold of the back of Uke's hand so that the thumb lies on thumb. The little finger is laid on Uke's pulse. Tori now turns a further 90° to the rear and at the same time he rotates the grip on Uke to his shoulder (see Page 145). Uke corrects his position to Tori. Uke's and Tori' feet are now all virtually on one line again.

Tori's free hand now grasps Uke's wrist and bends the arm at the elbow. Tori lowers his body deep into his knees and at the same time increases the pressure on Uke's elbow. This creates a lever on Uke's elbow and wrist. Uke gives in to this action by kneeling down on his rear knee onto the floor. His arm remains relaxed.

Grasping hold of Uke's elbow, Tori takes a gliding step behind Uke so that he can then turn round backwards 180° on his leading foot.

With his movement he brings Uke's shoulder down onto the mat.

So that he can control Uke, he brings his heels together and lowers himself. The photo is turned 90° to one side.

Finally, he kneels down so that Uke's shoulders are lying between his knees. His toes are propped up and his bottom is on his heels.

Uke's arm is laid in the joint of Tori's elbow. The other hand is pulling Uke's elbow towards Tori's upper body. Using a twist of the hips, Tori applies a lever hold on Uke's shoulder.

4.3 shomen uchi

irimi nage

The distance between Uke and Tori is such that Uke has to take an extra step in order to reach Tori. At the same time he lifts his diagonal hand and strikes downwards on Tori's head (see Page 279).

At that moment, Tori takes a step forwards and brings his forward arm up to control Uke's attack.

His arm glides down from Uke's elbow onto his lower arm without blocking the strike. By virtue of Tori's movement forwards, his own hand is now above his head and Tori is underneath Uke's strike (*irimi* – Chapter 2.3).

At this moment, Tori pivots round 180° backwards on his leading foot. The *tenkan* movement now releases the tension created by the *irimi*.

Tori controls Uke by the shoulder and brings him into a turning position. By using his knees to lower his body deeply, Tori brings Uke off-balance.

Uke follows this movement under control and supports himself by placing his hand down on the ground in order then to take a further step forwards (see Chapter 8.6).

In this position, Tori is standing as low as possible. His upper body is upright and his knees are tensed outwards. Tori is standing close to Uke and can keep him well under control.

Tori brings Uke's head onto his shoulder by bringing his throat or neck further down. At the same time, Tori brings his free arm upwards.

He now glides forward with his leading foot and finishes the movement of his arm by turning his thumb down and moving his arm in a circular motion downwards.

Uke kneels down on his inner knee and can roll over backwards.

soto kaiten nage

Uke and Tori are standing so far apart that Uke has to take a step to reach Tori. As he steps forward, he lifts his diagonal hand up over his head and strikes downward onto Tori's head.

At the moment that Uke starts his attack, Tori also takes a step forwards *(irimi)* and lifts his diagonal arm to control Uke's strike. Contact is made at about Uke's elbow level.

Tori lets Uke's strike glide past his arm and, at the same time, begins to control the elbow of Uke's arm with his free hand.

Tori sinks down deeply into his knees while keeping his upper body upright and tensing his rear knee outwards. Tori is now controlling Uke's elbow. His other hand moves round to the nape of Uke's neck and forces him to go down with this movement *(atemi)*. Uke similarly lowers himself deep down.

Tori's hand is on Uke's elbow and glides this down to Uke's wrist. Tori begins to turn round backwards pivoting on his leading foot.

The other hand carries on controlling Uke's head, and Uke now takes a step forward in order to give in to Tori's movement. Tori brings Uke's arm in an upward circular motion and as a result creates a lever hold on Uke's shoulder. At the same time he opens Uke's guard so that he can strike him on the head with his knee.

Tori levers Uke into a movement forwards by taking a gliding step forwards – Uke rolls away forwards.

4.4 yokomen uchi

ikkyo omote waza

Uke and Tori are standing so far apart that Uke has to take a step to reach Tori.

When taking this step he lifts his rear hand up over his head and strikes diagonally downwards at the side of Tori's head (*yokomen uchi* – see Page 280). The feet are in the mirror-image position *(gyaku hanmi)*.

At the moment that Uke begins his attack, Tori takes a step forward. At the same time he lifts his forward arm up to head height. The arm must be tensed sufficiently in order to control Uke's strike. Tori's rear hand also comes up over his head and controls Uke's longitudinal axis as he takes the step forward.

Tori begins to turn round backwards pivoting on his leading foot *(tenkan)*. The turning motion allows Uke's strike to be made but in an ideal case it is not very severe.

Uke adjusts the gap to Tori by making a gliding step and repositions himself so that he is opposite Tori.

As he turns Tori's hands come down. For this, the hand by Uke's head passes his (Tori's) body and goes underneath Uke's hand and back up again in a circular motion to Uke's head.

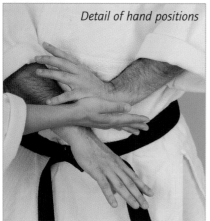

Detail of hand positions

Uke controls this movement by not being hit on the head. Tori's other hand grasps hold of Uke's elbow.

Tori now takes a step forward and finishes the movement by bringing his hands down.

At the same time, Tori's outer hand begins to grasp hold of the arm just above the palm. The other hand grasps hold of Uke's elbow.

Here, it is important that the movement is finished with a feeling of "closing" or cutting (and does not push Uke away).

In this position he controls Uke's shoulder. Tori now moves forward and outward in order to bring Uke down to the ground.

At the same time, his control on Uke's shoulder is firm.

Uke stays relaxed and gives way to Tori's movement.

So that Tori can hold Uke down firmly, he kneels down with his inner knee in the armpit of Uke's shoulder and the outer knee is on Uke's wrist. Tori's toes are propped up and his bottom is resting on his heels.

shiho nage ura waza

Uke and Tori are standing so far apart that Uke has to take a step to reach Tori.

When taking this step he lifts his rear hand up over his head and strikes diagonally downwards at the side of Tori's head. The feet are in the mirror-image position *(gyaku hanmi)*.

At the moment that Uke begins his attack, Tori takes a gliding step forwards and outwards.

The outer hand stops Uke's strike and the other hand controls his longitudinal axis.

It is important at this point for Tori to have a balanced position in which both arms can work equally as strong. The elbows are kept down and the arms are sufficiently tensed to be able to withstand Uke's strike.

Tori now brings his arms down in front of his longitudinal axis. At the same time he takes a gliding step backwards to give himself some room.

Tori pivots round backwards 180° on his leading foot, keeping his hands in front of his longitudinal axis.

Uke and Tori are now standing shoulder to shoulder. Tori has grasped hold of Uke's wrist in his outer hand.

Tori now takes a gliding step forwards again, at the end of which he lifts his arms a little and turns with his hips 180° underneath Uke's arm.

In this movement, it is crucial that Tori doesn't pull or lever Uke's arm. Tori moves through underneath the gripping point on Uke's wrist.

By virtue of Tori's movement a lever has now been created on Uke's shoulder and wrist.

Tori can now throw Uke by bringing his hands down to his leading foot thus concluding the movement.

Uke kneels on his inner leg and rolls over backwards.

If Tori finalizes the movement quickly enough so that Uke is not able to roll over backwards, then he is made to fall forwards over the pivot of his gripped wrist (see Chapter 8.4).

4.5 Application

The purpose of the few examples that follow, sketching out the working up process, – within the framework of the basic techniques in Aikido – was covered at the beginning of the chapter. One result of the work up process is the possibility now of using the knowledge gained. The term **'application'** means techniques that are directly realistic and take into account the principles of Aikido. We are not talking about a collection of 'various tricks', but rather about the application of the qualities that the *Aikido-ka* has learned and worked up by practicing the basic techniques.

In the following, we show some examples of movements for application:

jodan tsuki irimi nage

Uke attacks Tori with a *jodan tsuki* (see Page 281).

Depending on the position of the feet, Tori either takes a gliding step or a whole step forwards. At the same time, the hand on the mirror image side controls Uke's strike.

At the moment that Uke thinks he can hit Tori, the latter glides past the strike. Tori's inner hand is brought up directly into Uke's face.

Tori then takes another step forwards in order to bring Uke off-balance.

jodan tsuki hiji kime osae

Uke attacks Tori with a *jodan tsuki*. Depending on the position of the feet, Tori either takes a gliding step or a whole step forwards.

At the moment that Uke thinks he can reach Tori, the latter glides past the strike.

Tori's outer hand controls Uke's strike. At the same time, Tori lifts his inner hand up against the inside of the striking arm.

In the downward movement that follows, Tori would have had the opportunity to hit Uke's head. However, instead of this he brings his hand over the outer hand and then over Uke's elbow.

Both hands are then moved round 90° against Uke's elbow and bring it downwards. At the same time, Tori twists his hips round 90° outwards and accordingly changes the position of his feet (see Chapter 2.7).

Tori immobilizes Uke on the ground by using a lever on the elbow.

mae geri irimi nage

Uke attacks Tori using a *mae geri* (see Page 283). Depending on the position of the feet, Tori either takes a gliding step or a whole step forwards past Uke's foot.

At the same time Tori's hands can control Uke's leg.

At the moment of full tension, just as Uke is about to strike Tori, he glides past Uke's step.

Tori then brings Uke's head immediately onto his inner shoulder. Depending on Uke's stability, Tori can also additionally grab hold of Uke's hair.

This way, Uke is brought off-balance. At the same time, Tori's inner hand moves upward and connects finally with a technique at the side of Uke's head.

By executing this throw a lever is created over the nape of Uke's neck.

yokomen uchi ikkyo

Uke delivers a cross punch at Tori's head.

Tori takes a gliding step forwards and at the same time lowers himself down while keeping his upper body upright.

The hand on the mirror-image side begins to control Uke's punch without stopping it.

By using an upwards movement, the inner hand controls Uke's longitudinal axis and then crosses over Tori's other hand.

At the same time Tori begins to turn backwards pivoting on his leading foot. Throughout the attack Tori is standing, and because of his dodging movement is almost now behind Uke.

He grasps hold of Uke's arm and turns backwards further. At the same time he brings Uke's shoulder down on to the ground.

muna dori ikkyo omote waza

Uke wants to grab hold of Tori's lapel.

Tori begins to control the gripping action using his diagonal hand. At the same time he takes a step or a gliding step forwards and outwards to the side that Uke wants to attack.

His outer hand controls Uke's shoulder. At the same time Tori turns his hips through 90° – his foot (at the beginning the rear one) is now adjusted accordingly and is brought forward (see Chapter 2.7).

The hand on Uke's shoulder (angled at 90°) brings him off-balance.

Tori can now grasp hold of Uke's arm with both hands and bring Uke's shoulder down on to the ground to immobilize him.

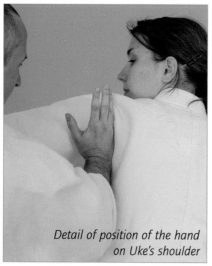

Detail of position of the hand on Uke's shoulder

Tori uses this movement shortly before Uke is able to grasp hold of Tori's lapel, but gives him every opportunity of being able to do it.

Generally speaking, Tori avoids letting Uke get a proper hold of him (wrist, shoulder or lapel).

"I don't know enough to be incompetent."

Woody Allen

5 Details of the Aikido Techniques

- Why are the details important?
- Why are the details a means to an end?
- What are the basic techniques?

All Aikido basic techniques *(kihon waza)* consist of exact laid down hand and foot movements. Of course, a complete technique is achieved first of all by looking at the whole of the sequence of movements. But it is also of note to have in your mind the fact that techniques are put together from a succession of specific detailed movements.

The details covered in this chapter are particularly important and should be of help in understanding each technique better. At the same time they are a characterizing factor in these techniques.

Principally, it is the whole movement that counts in the sequence of actions in a technique – detailed knowledge should make the flow simpler and not slow it down. If the sequence of movement is interrupted by the details then perhaps the correct moment has not yet arrived to devote particular attention to them. Should this occasion arise, the *Aikido-ka* has not yet reached the point – "zone of proximal development" (Lev Vygotsky) - where he can assimilate and work up a new detail successfully (see also Page 239).

Before we go on to cover the individual techniques, here are a few basic points:

- Holding and throwing techniques (*katame waza* and *nage waza*) are different. Both can also be combined *(nage-katame-waza)*. First of all, in this chapter, we cover the holding techniques (5.1 – 5.7), and then the throwing techniques (5.8 – 5.19).
- Many of the throwing and holding techniques can be done in front of Uke as well as behind him (*omote waza* and *ura waza*). Instead of *omote* and *ura*, sometimes one speaks of 'positive' and 'negative' techniques. This refers then, of course, only to the direction of the movement.
- When executing the techniques, Uke and Tori can be standing *(tachi waza)*, Tori can be kneeling and Uke standing *(hanmi handachi waza)* or both can be kneeling *(suwari waza)*. The technical details shown here are limited to the *tachi waza*. In part, the techniques change when done as *suwari waza* or *hanmi handachi waza*. To have covered every differentiation would go well beyond the scope of this book.

At the end of the individual basic holding techniques we will cover some advanced variations. This requires that the *Aikido-ka* has been practicing the basic techniques for a considerable time and can master them. In particular, Tori must be in a position to be able to move his feet flexibly. Moreover, he also has to have gained sufficient competence in executing his hand and arm movements, so that he can use them appropriately in the variations covered. Here, we are speaking about variations from the third phase of learning Aikido (see Chapter 7.1).

5.1   ikkyo

omote waza

The name of the first and most important holding technique in Aikido stems from *ichi* (= one) and *kyo* (= teaching) – so, *ikkyo* means the 'first teaching'. The aim of this holding technique is that by grasping hold of the elbow and the wrist just above the palm of Uke's hand, he can be brought completely under control and, finally, immobilized.

For the *ikkyo omote*, the distance between Tori and Uke is such that Tori can either grasp hold of Uke's elbow or alternatively punch him in the face.

By having these alternatives, Tori's movements, on the one hand, are made more plausible. On the other hand, the distance determines Tori's next move – i.e., he can close the gap by executing a downward cutting movement and taking a step forwards without pushing.

Using his grip on Uke's elbow and wrist, Tori's thoughts are to control and immobilize Uke's shoulder and keep the guard on the longitudinal axis. For this, he adopts a low stable position with his upper body remaining upright.

Control on the ground is achieved with his inner knee on Uke's armpit and the outer knee on Uke's wrist. The angle between body and Uke's arm is slightly more than 90°. Tori's toes are propped up, his bottom is resting on his heels and his upper body is upright.

Tori grasps hold of Uke's wrist just above the palm of the hand – his fingers are grasped around the wrist like a handcuff. He slides this 'handcuff' now along and outwards against the hand or the ball of Uke's thumb. Then he increases the pressure slightly by pushing his hand further outwards using his outer knee.

Imagine an *ikkyo* movement where Tori has a knife *(tanto)*: Uke controls the *tanto* by sinking down and controls Tori's lower arm. This way Tori cannot reach him – but at the same time, Tori can keep him under control.

ura waza

Tori is standing relative to Uke so that he can easily grasp hold of his elbow. The hand grasping the elbow is the one above Tori's leading foot.

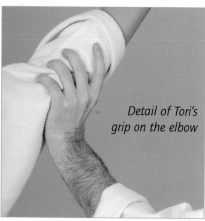

Detail of Tori's grip on the elbow

Tori grasps hold of Uke's elbow from below in such a way that the first contact is made with the little finger, the edge of the hand and the thumb. Tori can now turn round 180° backwards pivoting on his leading foot. The rotational axis of this movement is at about the height of Uke's elbow.

Tori is standing behind Uke's back and grasps hold of Uke's elbow as well as the arm just above the palm of the hand. Using this grip, Tori rotates Uke's shoulder so he can control the longitudinal axis of his guard.

Tori finalizes the movement by bringing Uke's shoulder down on to the ground. His outer hand is brought directly downward past his hips.

Tori controls Uke on the ground – his inner knee is on Uke's armpit and the outer knee is on the wrist. The angle between body and Uke's arm is slightly more than 90°. Tori's toes are propped up, his bottom is resting on his heels (see Chapter 2.9).

For some attacking moves (e.g., *gyaku-hanmi katate dori* or *kata dori* – see Page 275) in *ikkyo omote* and *ura*, Tori is grasping the back of Uke's hand. The little finger is held firmly on the pulse and the palm of Tori's hand is lying firmly on the back of Uke's hand. Uke's wrist is bent 90°.

5.2   nikkyo

omote waza

For the second holding technique (*ni* = two), a wrist lever is used in order to control Uke.

To change over from *ikkyo* to *nikkyo*, first of all Tori turns his thumb downward. The other hand brings Uke's elbow forward and downward. As he does, Tori rotates his thumb round Uke's wrist so he can change his grip without losing contact with Uke.

Detail of the hand position before the change

For this, Tori grasps hold of the back of Uke's hand with his little finger lying firmly on Uke's pulse. As in *ikkyo*, the other hand grasps Uke's elbow. Using the grip on the back of the hand or Uke's wrist, Tori rotates Uke's shoulder to control him.

As in the *ikkyo omote*, Tori brings Uke's shoulder down on to the ground to immobilize him. Uke relaxes and gives in to the movement.

Uke's arm is lying in Tori's elbow. The lower hand pulls the elbow towards Tori's upper body. The toes are propped up and the bottom is resting on the heels. By twisting his hips in the direction of Uke's head, Tori creates a lever on Uke's shoulder.

Nikkyo omote differs from *ikkyo omote* in its finish and in the fact that Tori can create an additional lever on Uke's wrist.

Variation:

An advanced variation of *nikkyo omote* is where Tori allows Uke to get up again and brings the gripped wrist up to his forward shoulder as Uke rises.

At the same time, the free hand glides past Uke's elbow and shoulder onto Uke's shoulder blade. By virtue of the movement of Tori's upper body forward and downward, a lever is created on Uke's wrist and in this way he is brought under control again. Differently to *nikkyo ura*, Uke's elbow is pointing up, because, here, it is an *omote* movement.

This variation requires Tori to execute continuous movement so that Uke cannot get into a stable position. Usually, Tori moves along a line towards Uke i.e, he doesn't move off the line like in the basic movement.

ura waza

In *nikkyo* ura, Tori systematically uses a lever on Uke's elbow and wrist to control him and bring him down to the ground. There can be three reasons for this:

- After turning round backwards for *ikkyo ura*, Tori is not in a position to bring Uke down on to the ground because the latter is too strong.

- Tori is already too far away from Uke before turning for an *ikkyo ura* - so he is not in a favorable position.

- Tori decides beforehand to use a lever.

Tori grasps hold of the back of Uke's hand so that his little finger is on Uke's pulse. The palm of Tori's hand is firmly lying on the back of Uke's hand. So that he has a fixed point for his grip, he brings it also up to his forward shoulder.

Tori's free hand grasps hold of Uke's lower arm in a way that his own elbow is lying on Uke's. Uke's arm is bent 90°, both at the elbow and also at the wrist

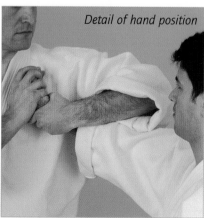

Detail of hand position

Tori now increases the pressure on Uke's elbow and creates the lever effect. In order for the movement to be effective, he lowers himself right down with his rear knee tensed outwards.

Uke gives in to the movement by bringing his rear knee down on to the ground. If he finds the movement too uncomfortable, he can slap the floor with his free hand – this is the signal for Tori to slack off the movement.

Tori then grasps Uke's elbow and controls it further with a firm grip on the wrist so that he cannot stand up again. At the same time, Tori takes a gliding step behind Uke with his leading foot.

Tori pivots round now on his leading foot 180° backwards and lays Uke on to the ground with this movement.

Tori kneels down in such a way that Uke's shoulders are between his knees. Uke's arm is trapped in the bend of Tori's elbow and the lower hand pulls the elbow towards Tori's upper body. Twisting the hips in the direction of Uke's head, Tori creates a lever hold on Uke's shoulder.

ai-hanmi katate dori nikkyo ura waza

If Uke attacks using an *ai-hanmi katate dori*, Tori is able to directly create a lever on Uke's wrist – here we are speaking about a special form of this technique. For this he starts the movement with a circular motion upwards in the direction of Uke's fingers.

At the same time, he fixes Uke's grasp by laying his free hand on Uke's fingers.

 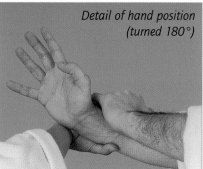

Detail of hand position (turned 180°)

At the same time, Tori moves off Uke's attacking line by turning his rear foot 45° outwards.

The hand, which Tori uses to grasp hold of Uke, is now over Uke's wrist. Uke's arm is bent at right angles both at the elbow and the wrist.

Tori brings his hands down in front of his longitudinal axis and thus creates a lever on Uke's wrist. Uke gives in to the movement by bringing his rear knee down on to the ground.

Tori grasps Uke's elbow and takes a step in order to then pivot round backwards on his leading foot. Using this movement he brings Uke's shoulder down on to the ground. Tori's inner knee is placed in the armpit of Uke's shoulder on the ground.

Tori's outer leg is lifted up. Tori is able to pull his hand out of the grip while still continuing to control Uke's elbow. He then grasps hold of the back of Uke's hand with his little finger placed firmly on Uke's pulse.

The same ending as in a *nikkyo omote* or *ura* now follows:

Tori kneels down in such a way that Uke's shoulders are between his knees. Uke's arm is trapped in the bend of Tori's elbow and the lower hand pulls the elbow towards Tori's upper body. Twisting the hips in the direction of Uke's head, Tori creates a lever hold on Uke's shoulder.

This form of the *nikkyo ura* can, for example, be used when Uke attacks with an *ushiro ryote dori* (see Page 285) and tries to grip too early in the beginning phase of the attack.

Nikkyo and all the following holding techniques can be used – as described above – if, by virtue of *ikkyo*, Uke cannot be controlled sufficiently enough. Therefore, Tori decides to employ an additional lever in order to control Uke.

If we imagine a case of an *ikkyo*, where Tori is controlling Uke by aiming a knife at him, then, for *nikkyo* the picture changes: Tori is not able to directly aim the knife at Uke. He, therefore, changes the position by bringing the blade round Uke's wrist and then he can control the wrist.

5.3   sankyo

omote waza

Tori is already controlling Uke with *ikkyo omote*.

He lets Uke's elbow go – Uke tends then to come upright again – but instead brings his upper arm or shoulder forwards onto Uke's shoulder.

At the same time, he lowers himself right down with his knees tensed outwards. With this movement, Tori temporarily prevents Uke from coming upright. Uke's arm is on Tori's (upper) body. Tori can now grasp hold of the edge of Uke's hand with his inner hand. The other hand grasps hold of Uke's fingers.

After this change, Tori takes a gliding step to the rear. Uke can now bring himself upright again.

With the grip on the edge of Uke's hand, Tori twists Uke's arm backwards and upwards and controls him this way. At the same time, Tori takes a step to the rear that now increases the twisting motion exerted by the lower hand. Tori's grip on the edge of Uke's hand controls him with the pivot axis being Uke's arm. Uke is forced back and cannot hold a stable stance.

Using the grip on the edge of Uke's hand, Tori brings Uke's elbow down and with his free hand he controls the distance between them *(atemi)*. At the same time, he begins to turn backwards pivoting on his leading foot.

Uke's upper body is brought downwards in this way. Using the twisting motion on the edge of Uke's hand, Tori keeps Uke under control further. The free hand moves to Uke's elbow. Tori moves further to the rear, pinning Uke's shoulder by the control over the arm and finally brings the shoulder down on to the ground.

Tori kneels down in such a way that Uke's shoulders are between his knees.

Tori now changes his grip and grasps hold of the edge of Uke's hand with his free hand so that he can keep up the twisting motion. The other hand pulls Uke's elbow towards Tori's stomach. By twisting his hips in the direction of Uke's head, Tori applies a lever on Uke's shoulder.

If the movement is too uncomfortable for him, Uke slaps the ground with the free hand.

shiho nage

Variation:

An advanced variation of *sankyo omote* is where, in *ikkyo*, Tori brings Uke forwards and downwards off-balance with a direct movement. As in the *nikkyo* variation, Tori does not move off Uke's attacking line.

Before Uke can adopt a stable position again, Tori's hand glides down to Uke's fingers and grasps them as in *sankyo ura* (see Page 157) – i.e., Uke can grasp hold of Tori's thumb.

Immediately using the grip, Tori twists Uke's elbow backwards and upwards. Uke adjusts his position to alleviate the pain.

With his other hand, Tori now grasps hold of the edge of Uke's hand without losing control over Uke's elbow. He finalizes this movement as in *sankyo omote*.

In this variation, it is important, as in all *sankyo* cases, that Tori keeps continuous control over Uke's elbow. Uke must not be given the opportunity of being able to pull his elbow backwards and downwards.

Detail of grip on the edge of the hand

ura waza

The sequence shown here begins in a position as given for example with a *shomen uchi* attack (see Page 279). Tori takes a step forwards and then turns round 90° backwards and increases Uke's movement downward. Uke adjusts his position relative to Tori. Both have their knees well bent and tensed outwards. The upper bodies are kept upright as far as possible.

Tori controls Uke's elbow, and with the other hand grasps the fingers so that Uke can get hold of his thumb.

Using the grip on Uke's hand, Tori now moves Uke's elbow upwards and twists his arm, tensing it.

At the same time as he carries out this upward movement, Tori's hand slips from the elbow down to the edge of Uke's hand. Tori grasps hold of the edge of the hand while Uke's elbow is still held in the tensed twisting grip so that he does not have the opportunity to pull it down.

The grip in sankyo ura

After this change of hands, Tori turns further to the rear *(tenkan)* and then he takes a step to the rear of Uke. By virtue of this step backwards, he brings Uke's elbow down. The free hand is then used finally to apply additional control over Uke's elbow.

(The sequence of movements is shown here from the other side (180°).

Tori turns further to the rear and thereby continuously increases the pressure on Uke's elbow and also the twisting tension on Uke's wrist. In this way he is brought down on to the ground.

Tori kneels down in such a way that Uke's shoulders are between his knees. Tori now changes his grip once again and grasps the edge of Uke's hand with his free hand, so that he can keep up the twisting tension. The other hand pulls Uke's elbow towards Tori's stomach. With a twist of his hips in the direction of Uke's head, Tori applies a lever on Uke's shoulder.

5.4　yonkyo

omote waza

Tori controls Uke as in *ikkyo omote* (see Page 138). He brings Uke's arm down in a circular motion by sinking down in his knees. Then he grasps hold of Uke's wrist and brings his elbow upward and forward with a circular motion.

As he executes the upward movement, Tori's upper hand slips from Uke's elbow directly down over his other hand.

Tori now grasps Uke's wrist and the lower arm in both hands and using this grip controls Uke's elbow. Tori's grasp is diagonal just as you would take hold of a sword.

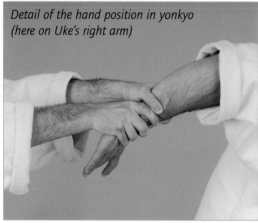

Detail of the hand position in yonkyo (here on Uke's right arm)

Using the grip, Tori controls Uke's elbow and thus Uke's longitudinal axis.

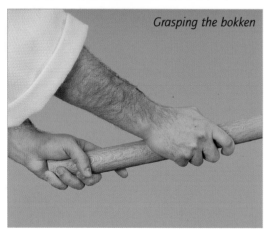

Grasping the bokken

The left hand grasps the end and right hand is grasping forward of this. The gap between the hands is about one hands width.

Tori now brings Uke's elbow forward and downward. He adopts a grip where the base of the forefinger of his upper hand is pressed down on Uke's lower arm. This can cause unpleasant pain. Tori moves further forward until Uke is lying down on the ground.

Tori's leading foot is pushed under Uke's shoulder and then Tori brings Uke's elbow forward and downward to pin him down on the ground.

ura waza

As in *sankyo ura*, the sequence shown here begins in a position as given for the example with a *shomen uchi* attack (see Page 279). Tori takes a step forwards and then, pivoting on his leading foot, turns round 90° backwards and increases Uke's movement downward and keeps his knees well bent.

Uke follows the movement and adjusts his position in relation to Tori – Uke's and Tori's feet are in line.

With his other hand, Tori grasps hold of Uke's wrist and controls Uke's elbow with his other hand.

Then, using the grip on Uke's wrist, he brings Uke's elbow upward and, as in *sankyo ura*, he creates a twisting tension on the arm to control Uke by the elbow.

While he executes the upward movement, Tori slides his hand along Uke's lower arm and grasps hold just above his other hand – as in *yonkyo omote* at a slight diagonal angle.

Tori pivots round on his leading foot, further backwards *(tenkan)*, until he is standing behind Uke.

Then using his grip on Uke's lower arm and wrist, he brings Uke's elbow upward in a circular motion and at the same time turns round further, bringing Uke down on to the ground.

Tori's leading foot is pushed under Uke's shoulder and then Tori brings Uke's elbow forward and downward to pin him down on the ground.

Variation:

An advanced variation of *yonkyo* is where Tori has changed over to *yonkyo* and is controlling Uke's elbow. Now, by using a direct movement onto the arm he can bring Uke off-balance and control his longitudinal axis.

It is important here that Tori does not pull Uke's arm, but uses the idea that by moving the whole of his body upwards as he controls the arm, Uke loses his balance. Tori lowers himself well down into his knees.

5.5   gokyo

gokyo – the *ikkyo* movement against an attack with a knife *(tanto)* – is traditionally only practiced in the *ura* form. In an *omote* movement there is the danger that Tori would not succeed in twisting Uke's arm enough so that the blade of the knife would be pointing away from Tori.

Uke attacks using *shomen uchi* or *yokomen uchi* and stabs *(gyakute)* (left) or cuts *(honte)* (right) at Tori's head

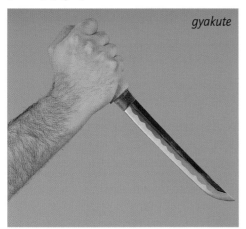
gyakute

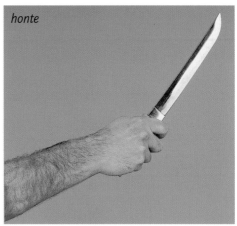
honte

Differently to most of the Aikido movements, generally in *gokyo*, Tori does not try to execute flowing movements but instead tries to stop Uke's attack as firmly as possible.

shomen uchi gokyo

Just as Uke starts his *shomen uchi* attack, Tori takes a step forward.

The hand to the rear first controls Uke's elbow. The forward hand takes the blow by slipping from the elbow to the wrist down along Uke's lower arm. Uke's attack is stopped this way. With his movement, Tori moves off Uke's attacking line slightly so that he can let the strike go past in a controlled manner and not get hit himself.

Tori grasps hold of Uke's wrist as near to the knife as possible so that Uke cannot move it further. His thumb is pointing upwards.

Detail of the hand position in the grip

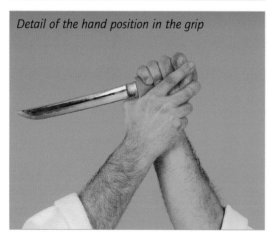

Then, Tori turns round backwards *(tenkan)* on his leading foot, and at the same time brings his arms down. With a firm controlling grip on Uke's elbow he is brought down to the ground.

Tori kneels down as in *ikkyo*: His inner knee is placed in Uke's armpit and his outer knee is on Uke's wrist. Uke's arm, however, is not laid down completely on to the ground. With his hand on Uke's elbow, Tori can exert a short pressure downward and make use of the counter-movement by Uke to push Uke's hand to his head and angle his arm.

Tori now exerts pressure again on Uke's elbow and creates a lever on Uke's wrist so that his grip is loosened and Tori can take the knife off him.

yokomen uchi gokyo

Uke attacks *yokomen uchi*. Just as Uke starts his attack, Tori takes a gliding step forward and outwards.

His forward hand stops Uke's strike and the other hand controls Uke's longitudinal axis *(atemi)*. Using this movement – just like in *shomen uchi gokyo* – Tori learns how to securely withhold and stop Uke's attack. In advanced practice, Uke should attack with ever more force but still in a controlled manner.

With his inner hand, Tori grasps hold of Uke's wrist as near to the knife as possible so that Uke cannot move it further.

Detail of the hand position

Tori brings his grip on Uke up in a circular motion and begins to pivot round backwards on his leading foot. At the same time his other hand grasps hold of the elbow.

As he turns, Tori brings his arms down. Controlling Uke's elbow firmly he brings him down on to the ground.

Tori kneels down as in *ikkyo*: His inner knee is placed in Uke's armpit and his outer knee is on Uke's wrist. Uke's arm, however, is not laid down completely on to the ground. With his hand on Uke's elbow, Tori can exert a short pressure downward and make use of the counter-movement by Uke to push Uke's hand to his head and angle his arm.

Tori now exerts pressure again on Uke's elbow and creates a lever on Uke's wrist so that his grip is loosened and Tori can take the knife off him.

5.6 hiji kime osae

This holding technique uses a lever *(kime)* directly applied to Uke's elbow *(hiji)*.

omote waza

First of all, Tori controls Uke as in *ikkyo omote*. To do this he adopts a firm stable stance with his upper body upright (see Page 138).

Tori grasps hold of the back of Uke's hand with his outer hand, such that his little finger is on Uke's pulse – this way Tori changes over to *nikkyo*. Tori uses his grip to twist Uke's arm far enough so that Uke's elbow is pointing forward.

Tori now lets go of Uke's elbow and brings his arm over and in front of Uke's arm. The hand grasps hold of Uke's wrist at the same time. His upper body is kept as upright as possible. He bends his knees well down with the rear knee tensed outwards.

Detail of Tori's control

Tori twists his hips and also his arm comes back and creates a lever on Uke's elbow. Uke is brought off-balance by this and gives in to the movement by moving back.

In order to finish off the technique, Tori can change over to *ikkyo* and bring Uke down on to the ground, or alternatively, kneel down with the inside knee and continue to exercise control over Uke with a lever on the elbow. The control being exercised at the end of the technique is the same for both *ikkyo* and *nikkyo*.

ura waza

The *ura* movement begins in the same way as the *ikkyo ura* – Tori doesn't grasp hold of Uke's elbow, though, but grasps Uke's wrist.

Tori takes a step forwards and pivots round backwards on his leading foot. At the same time he brings his own arm over Uke's elbow and begins to control Uke's shoulder this way.

Tori can now pull his hand away from Uke's grip and grasp round as in *nikkyo* (see Page 142).

The same view from the front.

From his low stable position, Tori turns his hips and thus his arm to the rear and in doing so creates a lever on Uke's elbow. Uke is brought off-balance by this and gives in to the movement by moving rearwards.

In *hiji kime osae*, it should be noted that Tori does not apply too much pressure on the lever on Uke's elbow to start with, otherwise Uke could easily block Tori's movements. On the contrary, Tori gets into position and then abruptly applies the lever but in a controlled manner. Because the elbow joint in this kind of lever is not able to give way anymore, this should be practiced with appropriate care.

5.7   ude garami

Uke attacks with a *gyaku-hanmi katate dori* posture and grip. Tori takes a gliding step forwards and keeps his distance to Uke by controlling it with his free hand.

The hand then moves to Uke's elbow and brings this in Tori's direction. At the same time, Tori's hand that is being gripped is moved in the direction of Uke's shoulder. This causes Uke's arm to be bent and his grip begins to loosen.

The edge of Tori's hand is now above the joint of Uke's shoulder. Tori begins to pivot backwards on his leading foot and at the same time moves his hands in a circular motion down past Uke's shoulder. In doing this movement, Uke's arm is wrapped round Tori's arm *(garami)*. At the same time a lever is achieved on Uke's shoulder.

Tori continues the movement further and brings Uke's shoulder down on to the ground. The same conclusion as in *nikkyo* follows (see Page 142).

Ude garami can also always be developed from the *kaiten nage* throw (see Chapter 5.11). At the moment that Tori has Uke under control, he doesn't move forward to throw him but then changes over to apply *ude garami.*

5.8 irimi nage

The idea behind irimi nage has already been explained (see Chapter 2.3). Here we show the conclusion of this technique.

Tori brings Uke's head onto his shoulder with his outer hand. At the same time he balances about 70% of his weight on his rear foot. Tori brings his inner arm up just slightly past Uke's head.

Tori turns his arm so that the thumb is pointing down. By virtue of this movement Tori's shoulder is rotated and this in turn creates a lever on the nape of Uke's neck.

During the movement, Uke remains normal and relaxed – and accepts Tori's movement giving in to it. The guard on his longitudinal axis remains i.e., he doesn't bend his upper body to the side. To make this possible, he raises his outside foot.

With a circular motion downward, Tori now begins to finish off the movement of his arm. Uke gives in to this movement by, first of all, placing his outer leg to the rear and then rolling over backwards over his inside leg. To make this possible, Tori lets go of Uke's head.

During *irimi nage*, Tori can bring Uke off-balance before he reaches the final position described above.

When Uke is brought down on to the ground completely, he lands on the lower arm and knee (see Page 300). This position permits Uke to stay compact and be able to react to Tori's movements.

Tori gets down right low with his rear knee tensed outward and his upper body kept upright. Tori keeps control of Uke by keeping contact with the elbow and shoulder blade.

sokumen irimi nage (naname kokyo nage)

Here we show the technique from the *gyaku-hanmi katate dori* attack. Tori takes a gliding step forwards and turns 90° outwards, pivoting on his leading foot.

At the same time he brings his hand onto his forward knee. Both squat down low. Uke can still hold onto Tori's hand. Both keep their upper bodies as upright as possible.

Tori now brings the hand that is being gripped up in front of his longitudinal axis and at the same time he brings his rear foot forward.

Tori then turns his hips round 90° in Uke's direction and moves behind him with his outside foot. Tori finishes off the movement by bringing his hand down to his leading foot taking Uke's head with it. As he does this he turns his arm so that he can see the palm of his own hand. The upper body is kept upright and Tori goes down well into his knees. Unlike in *irimi nage*, Uke's head is now kept on the outside of Tori's arm *(sokumen)*.

Using his free hand, Uke can control Tori's arm. When rolling down, Uke places his knee as far to the rear as possible so that he can absorb the energy from Tori's movement.

5.9   shiho nage

This throw can be executed in four different directions *(shi-ho)*. As a general rule, two versions are practiced – *omote* and *ura.*

For the movement, Tori moves underneath Uke's arm. It is important that as this is done, neither Uke's arm is pulled nor a lever created on Uke's elbow.

Tori does not rotate his elbows outwards but rather keeps them down into his sides. Tori grasps Uke's wrist as in a handcuff grip.

omote waza

After the first movements, Tori has grasped hold of Uke's wrist. He moves a pace in front of Uke and, at the end of the movement, lifts his arms and glides through underneath Uke's arm.

Tori then turns round 180° outwards *(tai no henka)*. By virtue of this movement, a lever is created on Uke's elbow.

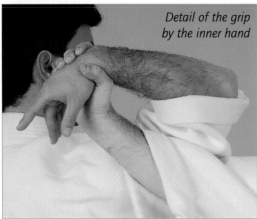

Detail of the grip by the inner hand

Tori now finalizes the technique by bringing his hands down to his leading foot. This movement passes just by Uke's shoulder – i.e., in a normal movement curve – and thus remains functional for the elbow of Uke.

Tori takes a short gliding step forwards and bends his upper body in the direction of his forward thigh in order to gain impetus by using his body for the throw.

Despite the lever, Uke keeps his arm and his shoulder relaxed and rolls over backwards.

ura waza

After the first movements, Tori has grasped hold of Uke's wrist. He takes a step forward from a diagonal position so that he can turn round 180° for the ura movement and so that Tori's and Uke's shoulders are at the same height *(tai sabaki)*.

Tori has grasped hold of Uke's wrist with his outside hand. His hands are in front of his longitudinal axis. Tori now takes a short gliding step forwards again and, at the end of this movement – like in *omote* – turns round 180°. Tori remains upright throughout the whole sequence of movements.

This way the same lever is achieved as in the *omote* movement. Tori finalizes the movement and can throw Uke with his technique.

The movements in the throw are similar to a cutting motion downward with a sword. The effect of the lever on the elbow remains as his hands come down directly past his own shoulder – there is no pull outwards.

When Tori increases the speed sufficiently that Uke isn't able to roll over backwards, then Uke falls forward over the axis of Tori's wrist.

5.10   ude kime nage

This throw is based on a similar starting movement as in *shiho nage*. In this example, Uke attacks with *ai-hanmi katate dori*.

omote waza

Tori starts the movement by placing his leading foot slightly outwards. His forward hand is still above his leading foot.

Tori then moves one pace in front of Uke. At the same time he brings his inner hand forward from the rear and twists his hand so that the thumb is downwards at the end of the forwards movement. This creates a lever *(kime)* on Uke's elbow *(ude)* and shoulder. This movement gives Uke a strong impetus forward and he rolls over forward.

When practicing advanced methods, Tori must ensure that his free arm increases speed on the forward movement.

ura waza

Tori grasps hold of Uke's wrist and pivots from a diagonal position into a position behind Uke *(tai sabaki)*. At the same time, Tori's grip on Uke's wrist is kept in front of his longitudinal axis.

Tori then takes a long gliding step forwards with his inside foot. Just as in the *omote* technique, at the same time he brings his inside arm forward and twists it so that the thumb is downwards at the end of the forward movement. This movement gives Uke a strong impetus forward and he rolls over forward.

When *ude kime* nage is correctly executed, Uke is not able to calculate whether Tori is going to strike at his ribs or his head with the forward movement. The throw is borne out of the feeling of the forward movement. For training purposes, if Tori is holding a knife in his hand, then the feeling will be particularly clear to Uke.

5.11   kaiten nage

In *kaiten nage* one differentiates between the forms of *uchi* and *soto*. First of all we show the *omote* movement for both techniques and then the *ura* conclusion for both.

uchi kaiten nage

Uke attacks with *gyaku-hanmi katate dori*. Tori takes a gliding step forward and outward and keeps the hand grasped still over his leading foot. His free hand controls the distance from Uke *(atemi)*.

Tori then takes a step inside underneath Uke's arm *(uchi)* and turns his hips round 180° *(kaiten)*.

Tori keeps his upper body upright throughout this movement.

Tori brings the hand being grasped down in front of his longitudinal axis and continues this movement with a step to the rear. At the same time he sinks down low in his knees.

Uke takes a step backwards giving in to the movement and bends his upper body down so that he can keep hold of Tori. Tori's free hand controls Uke's head *(atemi)*.

Tori brings his grasped hand up in a circular motion. This way he frees his hand and then grasps hold of Uke's wrist himself.

Tori brings his forward leg to the rear. Taking a step forwards, Tori creates a lever on Uke's shoulder bringing him forwards off-balance.

Uke keeps his shoulder relaxed and rolls over forward – one, because he is forced to do so by the lever on his shoulder and two, because he doesn't want to be struck by Tori's knees.

soto kaiten nage

Uke attacks with *gyaku-hanmi katate dori*. Tori takes a gliding step forward and keeps the hand grasped still over his leading foot. His other hand controls the distance from Uke.

Tori brings the hand being grasped upwards and outwards in a circular motion so that the edge of the hand is pointing at Uke. He then pivots 180° back round to the rear on his leading foot. Tori stays on the outside of Uke's arm *(soto)* (see Page 75).

The same movement as in the *uchi kaiten nage* now follows. Tori brings the hand being grasped down in front of his longitudinal axis and then takes a step to the rear while sinking down low in his knees.

Uke takes a step backwards giving in to the movement and bends his upper body down so that he can keep hold of Tori. Tori brings his free hand down at Uke's head *(atemi)*.

Tori brings the hand being grasped up. This way he frees his hand and then grasps hold of Uke's wrist himself.

Tori creates a lever on Uke's shoulder with a step forwards and brings him forward off-balance. Uke rolls over forward.

ura waza

After the starting movements of *soto* or *uchi*, Tori does not move to the rear but moves with a *tai sabaki* onto the front side and thus the other side of Uke's arm. At the same time he brings the hand being grasped down in front of his longitudinal axis. Uke bends his upper body over because Tori controls his head *(atemi)* with his free hand.

Tori moves forward with a gliding step from this position. He then takes a step and brings Uke's arm onto Uke's hip. This gives him the next pivoting axis for a further movement. Tori can now turn round back to the rear 180° so that he goes behind Uke's back *(ura)*. By virtue of this movement, Uke is brought off-balance.

At the end of the foot movements, Tori additionally twists his hips round 180° and brings the hand being grasped forward from the rear onto Uke's body so that he can throw him.

Uke follows through with the whole movement in order to avoid being struck on the head by Tori's knees and rolls over away forwards.

5.12   kote gaeshi

After the starting movement, Tori grasps Uke's wrist *(kote)* in his mirror-image hand. His little finger is on Uke's pulse and his thumb is on the back of Uke's hand. Using this grip Tori locks Uke's elbow.

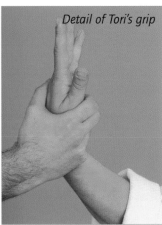

Detail of Tori's grip

Tori has adopted a position so that he can control the angle to Uke and at the same time execute a throwing movement past Uke's hips.

Tori uses his free hand for the throw, which he moves onto the back of Uke's hand and creates a lever on Uke's wrist (*gaeshi* = 'to turn, to change'). The direction of the movement is towards Tori's leading foot. Uke rolls away backwards or falls forwards over the axis of Tori's wrist when Tori increases the speed of the throw so that a backwards roll would be too slow.

Kote gaeshi is a so-called *nage katame waza* i.e., a throw that is finished off with a holding technique. Tori maintains his grip further on Uke's wrist after the throw. His free hand slides down to Uke's elbow and his thumb is pointing towards himself.

Tori moves his rear foot round Uke's head. Uke's wrist – still being held by Tori – remains covering over Uke's face. Using this movement, Uke is turned over onto his stomach.

The same ending follows as in *nikkyo*. Tori kneels down so that Uke's shoulders are between his knees. Uke's arm is pinned in the crease of Tori's elbow and Tori's free hand is pulling the elbow to his upper body. By turning his hips in the direction of Uke's head, he creates a lever on Uke's shoulder (see Page 142).

Second Option for kote gaeshi

Uke attacks with *gyaku-hanmi katate dori*. Tori brings his hand that is grasped up inside so that he can see the palm of his hand (see Page 79). At the same time he places his leading foot outwards to the rear and his rear foot comes forward. Tori is now no longer facing Uke frontally but stands at a 45° angle to him.

Tori's free hand grasps the ball of Uke's thumb from underneath.

 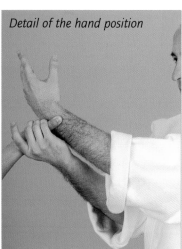

Detail of the hand position

Tori pulls his hand out of Uke's grip and brings it downward onto the back of Uke's hand. This again creates the lever on Uke's wrist. The lever is increased by Tori sinking down in his knees. Despite the lever, Uke keeps his arm relaxed and rolls over backwards or falls over forward.

The same movement seen from right angles.

5.13   koshi nage

Koshi means hips – so *koshi nage* means a series of throws using the hips – Tori throws Uke using his hips. There are several possibilities here. One thing is common in that contact with Uke is kept to a minimum as possible. In this way Tori avoids Uke holding on to him so he cannot start using a counter technique.

There is also a difference here to those hip throws seen in *Judo*. While in *Judo*, a groundwork holding technique should be used where possible, following a throw in Aikido you should have the opportunity to react to another attacker.

After the start of the movements, Tori has grasped Uke's wrist with his mirror-image hand and takes a step forward. Tori's free hand is controlling the distance to Uke *(atemi)*.

Tori brings his heels together and turns 90° towards Uke. His upper body is touching Uke's upper body. Uke grasps hold of Tori's jacket so that he can fall safely.

Tori sinks down into his knees, while at the same time keeping his upper body upright. He looks at his gripping hand and turns his hips slightly as he does this.

By sinking down low, Tori is now below the center of Uke's gravity. Tori's free hand is at eye level and it is now used to sweep towards Uke's legs. By virtue of this movement Uke is brought off-balance and falls down over Tori's hips (koshi). Tori lets go of Uke's hand so Uke can use it to slap the ground as he falls.

This learning form offers a good opportunity to develop the feeling for *koshi nage*. For training purposes, firstly, Tori can place his feet wider apart so that he can pick up Uke onto his hips slower. Uke must make sure he keeps relaxed but

not too slack. His upper body is not bent forward but remains as upright as possible so that he can fall down safely.

koshi nage from the basis of the shiho nage omote waza

This form uses the same starting basis as *shiho nage omote waza* (see Page 179). After Tori has started the movement, he grasps hold of Uke's wrist in his diagonal hand and takes a step forwards. He then brings his feet together and lowers his body.

At the same time, he brings his gripping hand up over his head and onto the other side of the body. He lifts his free hand up to eye level and begins to sweep in the direction of Uke's legs.

Uke is brought off-balance by this and falls down over Tori's hips. Because, in this throw, Uke cannot hold on, it is important that Tori maintains his grip on Uke's hand until the end of the fall.

koshi nage from the basis of the ude kime nage omote waza

This form uses the same starting basis as *ude kime nage* (see Page 183). After Tori has started the movement, he grasps hold of Uke's wrist in his diagonal hand. He then takes a step forward bringing his feet together in front of Uke and lowers his body well down. At the same time he twists his hips round 180°. His free hand moves past Uke's hips – but differently to *ude kime nage*, this movement is not done forward but upward.

Tori's free hand is now brought in a downward circular motion towards his feet. With his free hand, Uke grasps hold of Tori's jacket so he can fall down safely.

This movement causes Uke to be brought off-balance and he falls down over Tori's hips. Tori lets go of Uke's arm so that he can slap the ground as he falls.

koshi nage from the basis of the ikkyo omote waza

This form is based on the same starting movement as *ikkyo omote waza* (see Page 138). Uke attacks with *ai-hanmi katate dori.* At the beginning, Tori grasps hold of the sleeve of Uke's jacket at the elbow.

Tori then brings his feet together in front of Uke, lowers himself down well into his knees and twists his hips round 180°. With his free hand, Uke grasps hold of Tori's jacket so that he can fall down safely.

Tori brings Uke's arm, gripped at the hand and the elbow, in a circular motion downward. This causes Uke to be brought off-balance and he falls down over Tori's hips.

Tori lets go of Uke's arm so he can use it to slap the ground.

Dynamic Form

The *koshi nage* forms described above are more or less learning forms that can be used to work up the feeling for the *koshi nage* movements. In a dynamic attack, Tori does not have time to position himself at a 90° angle in front of Uke. This means that in a dynamic attack a dynamic form of *koshi nage* is required.

Uke attacks with *kata dori men uchi*. As Uke grasps hold of Tori's jacket at shoulder height, Tori has already moved further forward with his leading foot.

Tori controls Uke's strike with his forward hand and cushions the strike with his other hand.

By virtue of the forward gliding movements and the motion of Uke's strike, Tori is now standing level with Uke's hips. Tori begins to turn backward with his rear foot. Because of this movement and the dynamics of the forward motion Uke is brought off-balance and falls down over Tori's hips. For this, he lets go of Tori's shoulder and grasps hold of the jacket so that he can fall down safely.

For the execution of this dynamic form, it is important that Uke's forward movement is not interrupted and that contact between Uke and Tori is kept to a minimum. At the moment of contact, Tori is standing compactly in a low and stable posture and could strike Uke with his leading elbow.

5.14   tenchi nage

Uke attacks using *gyaku-hanmi katate dori*. Tori takes a gliding step forward and outward with his leading foot. At the same time his hand that is being gripped stays above his leading foot – i.e., it moves downwards (*chi* = earth).

By virtue of Tori's move forward, he and Uke are now level with each other. Tori brings his free arm up (*ten* = heaven) past the side of Uke's head. He then moves further forward with his leading foot and turns his upper hand round so that the thumb is pointing down. He brings his hand down towards his leading foot in a circular motion and finalizes the movement. This brings Uke off-balance and he rolls over backwards.

So he can fall down safely, Uke places his inside knee back as far as possible. If the movement is done correctly, Uke's head slips along past Tori's arm.

In a more direct and dynamic form, Tori can punch Uke in the face with his fist. The fist has the same trajectory as the movement with the stretched arm (see earlier). The tension in Tori's lower hand gives Uke the possibility of dodging and therefore not being hit by Tori. Uke then falls over the axis of Tori's hand.

5.15   sumi otoshi

Uke attacks using *gyaku-hanmi katate dori*. Tori takes a gliding step forward and outward with his leading foot. At the same time his hand that is being gripped stays above his leading foot.

His free hand moves up along Uke's longitudinal axis and controls the gap this way.

Tori brings his feet forward together and begins to sink down in his knees. At the same time his weight is balanced forward i.e., his bottom does not move to the rear. As he sinks down, his free hand slips down from above, along Uke's body and – having arrived behind Uke – in the direction of the knee.

This movement brings Uke off-balance. At the same time Tori sweeps Uke's legs away. Uke falls down forwards over the axis of the grip.

By kneeling down, it is easy for Tori to achieve the best angular position with Uke. In advanced forms it is then sufficient – if Tori can achieve this angled position, and by only kneeling slightly down – to bring Uke off-balance. On no account should Uke's grip be pulled as he will either pull it back, let it go or follow the movement sideways.

5.16   juji garame nage

Uke attacks Tori using an *ushiro ryote dori* (see Page 285). Tori lifts his outer hand and takes a gliding step rearwards through underneath Uke's arm.

At the same time he turns his outer hand inwards and grasps hold of Uke's wrist. Simultaneously, he brings his forward hand upwards to the rear in a circular motion and grasps Uke's other wrist in the fork between thumb and forefinger.

Tori crosses over Uke's arms *(juji garami)* and applies pressure.

 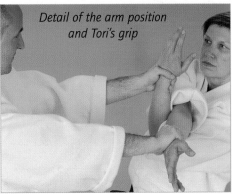

Detail of the arm position and Tori's grip

Taking a gliding step forward, the upper hand presses Uke's arm in a circular motion forwards and downwards. This brings Uke off-balance and he falls down forwards.

To fall over forwards, Uke has to sweep his rear leg away with his leading leg. Differently to other throws, in *juji garami nage*, it is not possible for Uke to be able to fall over forward and at the same time get away from Tori. Tori keeps hold of Uke with his inner hand and lets go with the other outer one so that Uke can slap the ground as he falls.

5.17   aiki otoshi

Uke attacks using an *ushiro ryo kata dori* (see Page 288). Before his attack is concluded, Tori takes a step sideways to the rear past Uke. At the same time his upper body remains upright and goes down well into his knees, which are tensed outwards. By virtue of this movement, Uke is brought slightly off-balance.

Tori can now brings Uke's knees together and grab round them with both hands.

This brings Uke right off-balance and Tori can lift Uke's feet and throw them behind him. Then Tori turns in the opposite direction so that Uke cannot pull him with him. Uke keeps hold of his grip on Tori's jacket with his rear hand, so that he can fall down safely.

5.18   kokyu nage

Kokyu means 'breathing' or 'exchange'. *Kokyu nage* are therefore Aikido throws that use the energy of the attack to bring Uke off-balance. *Kokyu nage* techniques are done generally with particularly dynamic and flowing movements and in which levers are not applied to Uke's joints. However, since all throwing techniques in Aikido posses the inherent sense of *kokyu nage*, you could call all throws *kokyu nage* ones.

Uke attacks with *jodan tsuki*. Tori cushions the punch with his diagonal hand. His other hand begins to control Uke's elbow (similar to *ikkyo omote waza*).

At the same time, Tori brings his rear foot forward as he meets Uke's punch. As he does this he keeps his upper body and head to the rear – in other words, Tori doesn't shorten the gap between them too much by virtue of his move forward.

At the moment Uke is about to hit Tori – i.e., at the moment of the height of the move and dynamics of the forward movement – he lowers himself into his knees, twists his hips through 180° and thus brings Uke off-balance. Thus the throw is achieved merely by Tori's dodging movement, without having to pull Uke's arm.

5.19   ushiro kiri otoshi

Uke attacks using a *chudan tsuki* (see Page 282). Tori takes a gliding step forwards and is able to cushion Uke's punch sideways with his leading hand without stopping his movement or blocking it (see Page 89).

Now Tori takes a further gliding step behind Uke's back and pivots on his leading foot 180° rearwards. At the same time, his hand begins to control Uke's head and chin from behind. Using his other hand, Tori does a cutting action downwards on Uke's head *(kiri)*.

Uke falls over backwards by sweeping his forward leg away with his rear knee. In this way he keeps moving forwards and is not struck by Tori.

5.20   suwari waza kokyu ho

As you read in Chapter 5.18, *kokyu* means 'breathing' or 'exchange' – 'ho' stands for 'exercise'. In *kokyu ho* it is a question of seeking to 'exchange' with Uke or exercise this principle (see Chapter 6.3).

The basic form for the exercise of this technique is as follows:

Uke and Tori squat down on their knees sitting opposite each other *(seiza)*. The toes are stretched out. Uke grasps hold of Tori's wrists.

Tori brings his hands up a little and pulls them both outwards opening up the area in front of Uke's chest.

He then brings the edges of his hands up to Uke's shoulders and causes Uke to go off-balance to the rear.

Position of the hands on the shoulders

213

Finally, Tori tips Uke to one side. Tori adjusts his position to Uke by following him down. At the same time he props his toes up. Tori now has control over Uke.

Uke keeps hold of Tori's hands and crosses his legs over so that he doesn't fall flat on his back.

In advanced exercises, Uke can attempt to keep hold of Tori and block him. Tori tries to maintain his posture and open Uke's guard and, despite the blocking movement, bring him off-balance.

For further reading:
Ueshiba, K & Ueshiba, M (2002) *Best Aikido: The Fundamentals*. Tokyo: Kodansha International Ltd.
Ueshiba, M (2003) *The Aikido Master Course: Best Aikido 2*. Tokyo: Kodansha International Ltd.

ikkyo omote waza

"Forgiveness is a virtue of the brave."

Indira Gandhi

6   Aikido is Based on Principles

- What are the main principles of Aikido?

- How can you learn the principles?

- How do the principles interact with each other?

All Aikido techniques are based on the same principles. These principles make the techniques into Aikido techniques and distinguish them from e.g., 'tricks' like those sometimes taught on self-defense courses. Principles are the constants that are always there even when the techniques are altered or put into use (application).

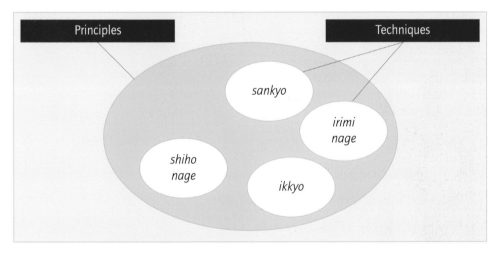

The aim of the learning process in Aikido is to recognize, understand, internalize and finally be able to use the principles. For this process, techniques in Aikido are a method of learning.

For the beginner in Aikido, it is sufficient first of all to take note of three principles:

- To recognize and be able to create the correct distance *(ma-ai)* to the opponent

- To be able to adopt the correct posture *(shisei)* – and of course...

- ...use the correct technique *(waza)*.

Concentrating on these three points will be challenging enough for the beginner in Aikido.

Advanced students of Aikido should make the effort to also take note, little by little, of the other principles in Aikido – e.g., being able to execute economical and pure movements and being able to ensure Uke's safety as well as one's own. At the same time as maintaining one principle, another one (principle) should not fall as a sacrifice. For example, if the *Aikido-ka* is only able to execute the correct technique by having to put too much power into it thereby losing his correct posture, then this is clearly wrong. In this case, the technique has been executed by giving up the principle of a correct posture.

Moreover, efforts should always be made to maintain all the principles thus achieving the execution of an ideal and perfect Aikido technique.

The following gives us a closer look (with examples) at the most important of the Aikido principles:

6.1   Correct Posture – shisei

The correct posture in Aikido looks like this:

- The upper body is upright (we speak of an upright longitudinal axis).

- The shoulders are relaxed and pulled back slightly.

- The head is upright in line with the longitudinal axis.

- The arms are held relaxed but not slackly.

- The feet are placed down in a line so that one is able to turn the hips and the feet on the spot without having to cross over the legs.

- The hands are held normally and ready for action hovering above the feet. The elbows are straight and generally not twisted or bent outwards.

shisei – sokumen irimi nage

hara

By practicing the correct posture you will develop a feeling for the central stable position of the body. In Aikido circles, the term of a 'stable hip' has crept into the language. The Japanese word for this is *hara*.

This term is of great importance for every martial art. By maintaining the correct posture and developing the feeling for a stable center, one gets a better feeling for the execution of movements with positive energy (see '*ki*' – Chapter 1). The movements are done relaxed but not slackly and they are done naturally and spontaneously. All of these three elements interact with each other.

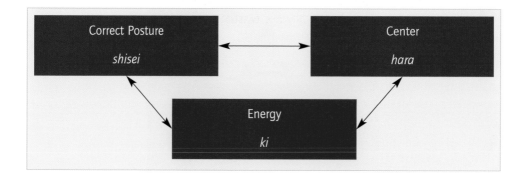

Correct Posture
shisei

Center
hara

Energy
ki

Several Aikido techniques require that you sink down low in your knees so that you can work with a lowered center of gravity. At the same time your upper body is kept as upright as possible and your knees are tensed outwards.

A further example of good *shisei* is when Uke attacks with *shomen uchi*, Tori does not bend over sideways but keeps his movements straight and upright. He cushions Uke's strike and can let him – thanks to his position and correct posture – slip past.

A further *shisei* example using a lowered posture is when Uke attacks with *ryo kata dori*. Tori stands upright with his knees well bent down. The leading hand controls the distance to Uke. Tori maintains a correct position despite Uke's attack. This fact allows him to control Uke's attack.

A correct posture is also essential when working with the *bokken*. This position holding the sword is called *hasso kamae*. Tori is standing upright in a balanced stable posture. This way he can effectively meet an attack or even he, himself, can rapidly and effectively attack.

6.2 Balanced Distance - ma-ai

"It's all to do with the right distance" – this remark by Christian Tissier reflects the importance of this principle. A firm figure for the right balanced distance between and Tori and Uke cannot be laid down. It depends, moreover, on which technique is to be practiced and the speed of its execution. The type of attack and of course the prowess of the people exercising also plays a role.

Tori is always responsible for the control of the distance to Uke because he is the one who has to defend himself. "Control" means in this context that Tori always has time to react appropriately to Uke's movements and avoid being surprised.

Particularly, when one is beginning to learn Aikido, it is always sensible to practice first of all with a slightly larger distance between the two. This means that Uke always has to take an extra step to reach Tori for the attack. When you reach a higher level, it is possible and more meaningful to practice closer together. In that case, Uke will only need to take one gliding step forwards to attack Tori.

When working with the *bokken*, the meaning of the distance between Uke and Tori becomes very important. If Uke and Tori are standing opposite each other with swords in a *seigan kamae* middle guard position, they are at the same distance from one another as in the basic technique in Aikido. Both can reach each other and also control each other. If the distance were greater, there would be no danger for either of them, because they couldn't hit each other without really making some effort. If they were closer together they could no longer control each other and they would be in a position to surprise the other

6.3   Searching for Exchange – aiki

Ai means harmony, a bringing together and the unison in harmony – *ki* stands for energy. Together, *aiki* refers to the principle that the initial opposing energies of Tori and Uke are united and brought into harmony (see Chapter 1). For the exercises, this means that Tori must not block Uke's attack, but rather take up the movements or even anticipate them and move with them. In this way, Uke becomes a physical as well as a mentally attuned, communicating partner. This permits a harmonized blending *(kokyu)* between Tori and Uke.

However, this is assuming that Uke is disposed to recognize such a situation. If he shuns Tori's approach, the Aikido techniques can injure him. Thus it can be seen that Aikido is based also on deterrence and insight.

Following his attack, Uke gives way, otherwise Tori could injure him

The more Tori has been trained, the more he can refrain from exercising sanctions with the Aikido techniques, because he can still also control the distance between them even if Uke is not prepared to accept harmonization.

Fundamentally, the Aikido techniques can be characterized as true techniques that have been developed expressly to open the door for this harmonization. Similarly, they have not been conceived for fighting against an opponent. These thoughts have been manifested in the Aikido techniques. An example par excellence for this can be seen in the exercise *kokyu ho*.

kokyu ho

Uke attacks Tori with *katate ryote dori* (see Page 276). Using his technique, Tori attempts to mix in with Uke's grasping actions, without pulling or pushing.

For this he brings his leading foot to the rear and outwards and places his rear foot forward where his leading foot was before.

By virtue of this movement he leaves the original line between himself and Uke and is now standing at a 45° angle to Uke. He leaves the arm grasped by Uke in front of his longitudinal axis. Tori sinks down low in the knees thus bringing his center of balance below the point where Uke has him in a grip.

Tori can now bring his arm upwards along his longitudinal axis.

When his arm is over his head, Tori twists his hips, takes a step behind Uke and finalizes the movement by bringing his hand downwards in a circular motion in the direction of his leading foot.

This leads to Uke overbalancing and rolling over backwards.

kokyu ho (Second Option)

The same exercise can be done in a different form. Uke attacks as in the first form with a *katate ryote dori*. Tori pivots round 90° to the rear on his leading foot and brings the arm being gripped towards his leading knee. At the same time he sinks down low in his knees.

Tori then brings his hips even lower down so that the hand being gripped by Uke is tipped upwards.

Tori can now bring the hand being gripped back up again along his longitudinal axis. At the same time he brings his rear leg forward.

When his arm is over his head, Tori twists his hips around about 180° in Uke's direction and, using a gliding step, comes behind Uke. He then finalizes the movement again by bringing his hand downwards in a circular motion.

Uke is brought off-balance and rolls over backwards.

6.4   Maintaining a Guard

A basic principle in any martial art is to maintain your guard so that Uke cannot exploit any opening in it. First of all, in Aikido this means – in expectation of an attack – Tori's guard is open. The longer Uke takes for his attack, the more Tori closes his guard by increasingly controlling the angle between himself and Uke. On the grounds of this concept, in Aikido there is no particular guard position at the beginning of a technique.

At the moment that Uke reaches Tori, the latter's guard is completely closed. During the further movements, Tori strives to make sure that he doesn't leave any openings. Therefore, in an ideal case, there is no follow up attack by Uke, because immediately after the first contact, he is being controlled by Tori.

In the following example of movements, Uke attacks with *gyaku-hanmi katate dori*. Tori takes a gliding step forwards and outwards. Tori's hand that is being gripped remains above his leading foot.

Tori's rear hand closes the guard position by controlling Uke's longitudinal axis.

By virtue of this, Uke is pinned for a moment. The gap between Tori and Uke is such that Tori could strike Uke. The movement has proved to be reliable. If Tori's position is correct, Uke cannot reach him with his free hand.

The same start can be executed at a higher level of training: Uke attacks dynamically. Tori slips his body round past his wrist being held by Uke.

His arm is lying against his body and he turns the edge of his hand down as he glides forward – the idea being that he is cutting upwards at Uke's body. Again, the free hand is controlling Uke's longitudinal axis at the neck.

Uke leaves his arm stretched out, because if he bent it in, Tori could reach him with his free hand. At the same time, Uke, by virtue of his grip, controls Tori's other hand.

6.5   Working with Axes and Angles

In all Aikido techniques, one works with the concept of axes and angles. The concept sees Tori and Uke having their own longitudinal axis with a central point *(hara)*. Besides this is the angle they adopt when opposing each other (this is usually between 0°-45° in the starting position) and then there is also a rotation point.

From a bird eye's view the concept looks like this:

Tori moves always in relation to Uke's longitudinal axis (i.e., not in relation to his arm or wrist) and tries to control the angle between himself and Uke. At the same time, Tori has to find where the rotational axis is for the technique.

This principle is shown clearly in the following example: Uke attacks with *ai-hanmi katate dori*. Tori and Uke both have their longitudinal axes with their center. The rotational axis is at the point where Uke is gripping.

After Tori has freed himself from the grip (see Page 71), he can turn himself round with *tai-sabaki* using the axis of Uke's grip.

In this example, establishing where the rotational axis lies is relatively simple, because Uke doesn't move. The challenge is when the exact rotational point has to be found quickly and precisely during dynamically executed movements. Only this way can pulling and pushing movements be avoided.

In the second example, Tori and Uke are standing on the same line opposing each other.

Uke attacks with *shomen uchi*. Tori glides forwards and outwards off the line of Uke's attack. His leading arm is brought at the same time upwards up his longitudinal axis. Contact with Uke is carried out on Uke's elbow. Tori's hand slides up Uke's lower arm while his other hand grasps Uke's elbow.

Detail of the position of the feet

Starting like this, Tori has moved so that the line-up of his feet is pointing at Uke's longitudinal axis. In other words, Tori has adjusted his position to Uke so that he can work effectively.

It will be difficult for Uke to move his arm away, because there is a danger that he will be struck by Tori's upper hand. The angle between Tori and Uke is about 45°.

6.6   Learning Pure and Economical Movements

Do means way. As seen in Far Eastern eyes, this has the sense of working on the technique as a method for oneself (see Chapter 1).

However, the technique only becomes a method or tool for so-called mental work if it is practiced in order to perfect the technique itself in the first place.

The ideal technique is one where the sequence of movements is carried out as economically as possible and where everything that is superficial as a result − i.e., everything that is not absolutely necessary for the execution of the technique − is left out. In this sense the technique can then be called a 'pure' technique.

With this in mind we arrive at the following paradox: The simpler a movement is, the more difficult it is to execute it. This is because it is always more demanding to achieve further improvement in such a technique. In this sense, you will experience many years of captivating development possibilities.

As an example of this principle, we show the following movement exercise: Uke attacks *chudan tsuki*. Just at the moment that Uke thinks he can hit Tori, Tori takes a gliding step forward past Uke's strike. As he moves forward, without swinging it at all backwards, Tori lifts his forward hand up along a direct line past Uke's head.

Uke spots this 'pure' movement at the last second and, as a result, cannot block it.

Tori brings his leading arm downwards in a circular motion and concludes the movement. Uke is brought off-balance and rolls over away backwards.

6.7 Maintaining One's Own Integrity and Preserving That of the Opponent

In all Aikido techniques there is a common factor that they all have the same aim of maintaining Tori's integrity. This means in other words: Tori is not struck by the attack, but – thanks to his technique – can protect himself.

As opposed to other martial arts or martial sports, great importance is attached to Aikido in ensuring that Uke's integrity is also maintained as far as possible. This will be successful when Tori uses his defensive techniques appropriately and takes care not to injure Uke or only cause an injury when Uke's actions make it otherwise impossible to avoid. This idea has to be understood as a concept, valid for any form of practice or exercise.

Maintaining the integrity of the attacker, moreover, means that Tori has to proceed so that by virtue of his actions, Uke is not provoked. This is another clear indication of why there cannot be any form of competition in Aikido. If Tori were to attack first, then the principle of maintaining integrity would not be taken into account.

Here is an example of this principle: Uke attacks *men uchi* (see Page 281).

Tori cushions the attack with his leading hand and then glides with one step forward past the point of contact and pins Uke's shoulder with his free hand.

Both note where the point of contact is with their hands. If Uke were to quit the point of contact, he would run the danger of being struck in the face by Tori's hand. At the same time, however, Tori controls Uke's arm so that Uke cannot start a fresh attack.

In this position, Tori is protected from Uke's attack i.e., his integrity is maintained. At the same time, Tori gives Uke the opportunity to understand what has happened in this movement so that Uke is not injured – thus maintaining Uke's integrity.

6.8   Intention, Decision and Action - ki-ken-tai

One aim of Aikido training is to bring body and mind together in unison. What does this mean?

When Tori is attacked, he could have the aim to counter Uke's attack in a particular way (using his technique). This aim must be seen in correct comparison to his ability. If Tori misjudges his possibilities e.g., because of a lack of experience, then the execution of the aim is not achieved.

Tori could already intend to carry out a particular action without having decided when the action (i.e., the movement) should be done. This is where Tori has to find the correct moment in time. If he has a realistic aim and Tori chooses the correct moment, then the body action follows.

Body and mind are now in unison when these three elements – aim, decision and action – consistently come together. Therefore, for example, an action carried out by Tori that has not been preceded by a distinct, proper decision will be hesitant and indecisive. If a decision is not made at the correct moment then the timing of the movement will not be right. If his aims are well above his capability, then an action that stems from this situation will – as an aim – constitute only a dream.

Bringing the hurdle of matching intention, decision and movement into unison is made all the more difficult by the fact that these three elements cannot be executed all at the same speed. Thus our intentions – the *ki* – are practically unlimited and are just as rapid. In his thoughts, Tori can be immediately with Uke as soon as he attacks. If a decision to act springs from the intention, then the movement of the body can begin. In this, Tori's hands or sword – *ken* – can move quicker than the rest of the body. Thus, in first place are the thoughts or 'the mind' *(ki)* followed by the decision and the hands or the sword *(ken)* (that are on the periphery of the action) in coordination with the whole of the body *(tai)*.

The skill is to be able to use the sequence *ki-ken-tai* as naturally as possible. Paradoxically, the beginner in Aikido, however, first of all learns a sequence of movements in which all three elements interact at the same time so that he is in a position to be able to execute a basic movement at all. This means, for example, that the movements of the arm or sword are artificially slowed down so that the body can be brought into play, although, in reality, they could be naturally done much faster.

Many long years of training are necessary to learn how to use the three elements of intention, decision and action in a natural way and then move the body in a manner so that, for example, the hands are faster than the body, nevertheless allowing everything to interact correctly.

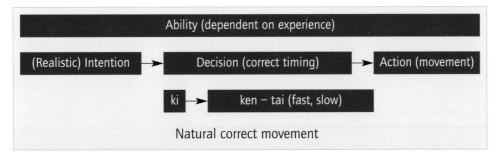

Ability (dependent on experience)		
(Realistic) Intention →	Decision (correct timing) →	Action (movement)
	ki → ken – tai (fast, slow)	
	Natural correct movement	

Intention, decision and action in perfect unison – Christian Tissier and Pascal Guillemin: irimi nage

"An idea that is developed and put into action is more important than an idea that exists only as an idea."

Buddha

7   **Learning Aikido**

- How do you learn Aikido?

- How does freedom of movement come about?

- What is an ideal technique?

- What is 'application'?

In this chapter, we are going to go into what the particular Aikido learning process is all about. But, first of all here are a few general considerations. How do people learn? For this question there are several bookshelves of literature on hand – but here are a few basic facts that are interesting for Aikido instruction:

- Learning will be particularly successful whenever new knowledge is coupled with something already known. This calls for a systematic gathering of knowledge and a structural build up of the Aikido instruction. A 'good' instructor will recognize where the corresponding student has reached in his development and what information he can already connect to with his existing knowledge. Previously (see Page 137), in connection with this, we spoke of the "zone of proximal development". Giving the student random information about this or that and to impart any old tip or other will have little promise of success.

- The exercisers must have the opportunity to be able to absorb, consolidate and revise what they have learned. Newly acquired knowledge has to be honed. Therefore, rapid, systematic changes of topic during an Aikido lesson are not to be recommended.

- Part of the process is to be able to learn without having any fear. Modern research into the psychology of learning has established that there is a coupling of emotion in the learning process with the content of what is actually learned. When what has been learned is used, the emotions that were felt when learning come back to light.

  Any feeling of fear and the possibility to exercise creative thinking or solve problems counteract against each other. So if the learning process was coupled with fear, then there is the danger that what was learned will not be used intelligently or be of any profit.

- Learning can be made particularly successful when not only the content of what has been learned can be digested but also at the same time mulled over and the whys and wherefores of why such things were learned reflected upon. This is called metacognitive learning – i.e., 'knowing about knowing' and thinking about the learning process itself. This speaks for a well thought through and a logically understandable concept.
- The learning process takes place in a small extent of the area between boredom and overtaxation – the term for this is "flow". If the students exercising get the feeling that the same thing is being said and instructed over and over again, then boredom creeps in. Similarly, if the selected topics strain and overtax the students and they are too difficult, the interest and the emotional intake wane and fall away.

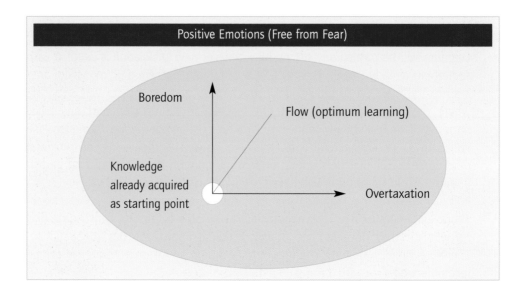

Further Reading:
Csikszentmihalyi, M & Jackson, S (1999) *Flow in Sports* (Human Kinetics)
Hannaford,C (1995) *Smart Moves: Why learning is not all in your head.* Great Ocean Publishers)
Csikszentmihalyi, M (1990) *Flow – The Psychology of Optimal Experience* (Harper + Row)

Christian Tissier and Bodo Roedel: ikkyo ura

7.1   The Three Phases of Learning in Aikido

All the basic techniques in Aikido follow precisely laid down movements that the *Aikido-ka* has to learn. Hand and foot movements are not done just as you like and only vary slightly, dependent on the exercise partner's physical characteristics. For example, a larger built partner *Aikido-ka* will of course move a little differently to one who is built smaller.

Learning the techniques will always ideally follow the same sequence:

One begins with the static construction of the technique. Little or no dynamics is used. Uke acts passively as far as possible – he becomes the static point of reference for Tori's movements. Tori learns the exact hand and foot movements from a static starting position. It is Tori who carries out the main part of the movements with Uke hardly moving.

The next step is done with more dynamic and where Uke and Tori begin to move more together with each other. In this phase, each carries out about 50% of the movement. Uke uses a dynamic attack. For this, the gap between Uke and Tori has to be big enough so that Uke has to take a step forwards for his attack. Both learn the Aikido techniques in this constructive 'pro and contra' mutual process. Simultaneously, a feeling is developed for the flowing and harmonious movements, done without a pause. Similarly, a good feeling for the correct gap between them is created. Uke and Tori improve their actions mutually and get to learn the Aikido principles and eventually internalize them.

The third phase is opposite to the first: Tori becomes continually, more and more, the center point of the movements. He moves Uke round this center point. Whereas in the first phase, Uke moved less than Tori, the weighting of the amount of movement is now different. This is, of course, dependent on the Tori's prowess and his ability to have internalized the Aikido principles.

Of course, a differentiation between the three phases doesn't occur in training in such a typical way. Beginners sometimes can move dynamically right from the start, although they are hardly able to carry out the static exercise movements. Advanced students do the static movements slowly in order to check the correctness of their technique and its details. Nevertheless, the differentiation portrays the conceptual background of Aikido.

For the *Aikido-ka*, each phase of learning is important for him to visualize what he is exactly practicing and why some movements are static and on the other hand some dynamic and generally how these factors change the techniques.

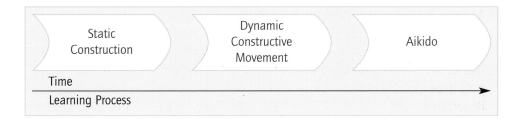

7.2   Aikido as a Way of Learning Freedom of Movement

Firstly, as we have already said, you learn Aikido using laid down forms of movement. The Japanese term for this is *kata*. By virtue of the *Aikido-ka* practicing the hand and foot movements and getting them to become routines, at the same time he internalizes the individual techniques. In the end the *kyu* tests (see Chapter 9.3) serve this very purpose of understanding the system of Aikido, and step-by-step, the *Aikido-ka* learns the individual techniques and at the same time discover the principles behind them.

This is followed up with the work on the techniques: What we call "Working up Techniques" (see Chapter 4). The techniques are used in order to 'build up' the body in a specific Aikido sense and manner. The characteristics of the interplay between Tori and Uke can be basically summed up also as an exchange of questions and answers: How stable are my arms when Uke really strikes? How stable is my posture when Uke attacks fiercely? Is it possible to actually stop Uke, lead him and throw him? If the *Aikido-ka* is, at first, perhaps still nervous about being struck then the 'working up' sessions – thanks to the techniques – allow him the opportunity to gain confidence and thus lose his fear of working up a particular movement. As indicated earlier, freedom from fear is an important basic requisite of being able to use one's knowledge sensibly.

The feeling for a stable posture is worked up in this way and the *Aikido-ka* learns how to employ his posture to bring Uke into the correct position. At the same time he continues to internalize the principles of Aikido. When placing this process of learning better knowledge in relation to the grading tests, this leads to the work for Grades 1st – 4th *dan* (see Chapter 9.3).

If Tori carries on practicing the laid down sequences of movements of the basic techniques *(kata)*, then he opens up a series of ideal situations to leave these laid down sequences of movements behind him and move on to develop freedom in his

243

movements. This means that he can still use his Aikido techniques with a partner, who does not keep to the prearranged agreements reached which are necessary for learning the *kata* (see Chapter 8.2). In an ideal situation, Tori positions himself straight away so that Uke has no idea that the technique is theoretically ended before he realizes it.

Again, we have an example of the characteristics of Aikido: Effectiveness in Aikido doesn't mean having to employ one's own strength against Uke's attack and the energy that evolves from it, but to end it by using a pure technique that is true to the principles of Aikido. Uke's attack ends in a vacuum because he doesn't meet any resistance that he can exploit for his own means.

Of course, the development of formal *kata* through to free movement, in reality, is not seen to nor does it follow a strict sequence, just like in the three phases of learning mentioned earlier – rather it represents a typical and ideal succession of events and forms the background concept for Aikido training.

7.3   Ideal Techniques and Application

In order to thoroughly understand Aikido, differentiating between learning an ideal technique and the use of Aikido techniques is very important.

In the learning process, the *Aikido-ka* tries to improve the techniques to such an extent that he also tries to take all the principles of Aikido into consideration. By definition, being able to achieve a perfect technique in Aikido is unfortunately virtually impossible, because when executing one, a new mistake or so will always crop up. However, since it is not to do with a real fighting situation, the *Aikido-ka* – when carrying out each movement - has the opportunity to avoid mistakes made and recognized, and slowly make improvements this way. In time, he makes fewer and fewer mistakes and can slowly make advances in his efforts to get near to executing an ideal technique.

Within the framework of the working up of the techniques, the learning process is based on certain pre-agreed arrangements between Uke and Tori (see Chapter 8.2). Thus Uke supports Tori by keeping to what has been agreed so that the techniques can be learned and the principles discovered.

The constructive character of the agreements make it, once again, clear that the basic techniques in Aikido are not effective in the sense of any real usage – they have not been constructed with the aim of acting against Uke. Their whole purpose lies solely in permitting Tori to advance in his learning process. First, when Tori has developed sufficiently to be able to use the principles of Aikido extensively, he is able use the Aikido techniques realistically. At that point, Tori will no longer be reliant on Uke's cooperation and will be able to execute these techniques (see further information on the topic of application in Chapter 7.5).

7.4   Examples of Movements

In the following two examples of movements, we show how the previous passages come into play. For this, the techniques are gone through in the static form (first learning phase), and then in the form where Uke and Tori move together (second learning phase). Finally, we show the form where Tori is the central point and Uke is moved around this point (third learning phase).

gyaku-hanmi katate dori ikkyo omote waza

First phase: Uke and Tori are standing opposite each other in a mirror-image position. Both have adopted a stable starting posture with the leading knee bent and the upper body upright. Uke grasps hold of Tori's wrist.

Tori brings his feet forwards together and controls the gap with Uke with his free hand (see Chapter 2.2). The knee is kept bent i.e., Tori doesn't lift himself up in this movement. Uke doesn't move and neither pushes nor pulls – rather he is the relative point for Tori's movements.

Tori now places his other leg to the rear. At the same time brings his free arm onto Uke's elbow. As he does this he doesn't pull Uke rearwards thus towards him, but rather makes him go down a little by the movement so that he can pin him. Uke gives into this impulse and corrects his distance to Tori with his leading foot. He sinks down low so that his upper body can remain upright.

The hand being gripped by Uke has not moved and is pointing at Uke's face. Tori now lets this hand drop and at the same time grasps the back of Uke's hand in his other hand.

Tori moves this hand in a circular motion upwards while, with the other hand he grasps Uke's elbow directly.

Tori takes a step forwards, brings his hands in a circular motion downwards and thus finalizes the movement. Uke's upper body is bent over. Moving over his grip on Uke's elbow and wrist/back of the hand, Tori can now control Uke by pinning his shoulder.

Now Tori takes a step forwards and outwards and brings Uke's shoulder down to the ground.

In order to control Uke, Tori kneels down. His inner knee is lying on Uke's shoulder and his outer knee on his wrist. Tori's toes are propped up and his bottom is touching his heels.

Second phase: Tori and Uke each carry out about 50% of the movements – the sequence will now become more dynamic. Uke attacks by taking a step forwards and again grasps hold of Tori's wrist.

At the same time, Tori takes a step forwards thus controlling the gap to Uke with his rear hand. The hand is now not brought fully to Uke's face. It stops at a point where Tori can move Uke's elbow following Tori's turn to the rear thus causing Uke to lose his balance.

Tori has now carried out the same footsteps as he did in the first phase. However, he is now a full step forward and has turned round to the rear – *tai sabaki* (see Chapter 2.5).

The same position seen at a 90° angle.

Uke follows Tori's movement by correcting the distance with his forward foot. The rear leg turns at the same time. In relation to Tori, Uke adjust his position so that he can continue with his attack.

Before this movement comes to a halt, Tori grasps the back of Uke's hand or his wrist. He brings his hand upwards in a circular motion while his other hand grasps hold of Uke's elbow.

Uke adjusts his position further towards Tori with the intention of reaching him with his free hand. Tori takes a step forwards and brings his hands in a circular motion downwards. This finalizes the movement.

This causes Uke to come off-balance and therefore he has to touch the mat with his free hand, while his forward foot moves upwards to compensate being off-balance.

Using his grip on Uke's arm, Tori now controls Uke and pins his shoulder. Before Uke can stabilize himself again, Tori takes a further step forwards and outwards and brings Uke's shoulder down on to the ground.

In order to control Uke, Tori kneels down. His inner knee is lying on Uke's shoulder and his outer knee on his wrist. Tori's toes are propped up and his bottom is touching his heels.

Third phase: Tori, acting as the center point brings Uke round. Uke attacks by taking a step into a *gyaku-hanmi katate dori*. This time, Tori takes a step backwards – here he also changes the side of the body.

With the movement to the rear Tori lifts his arm that is being gripped by Uke, up a little. At the same time, with his free hand, he grasps the back of Uke's hand or his wrist.

At the same time as Uke comes forward, Tori brings the back of Uke's hand to his shoulder and creates a lever on Uke's wrist.

Tori can now control Uke using the grip on his wrist and elbow and applies an *ikkyo*.

gyaku-hanmi katate dori
soto kaiten nage

Firstly, again we show the **first** static **learning phase.** Uke attacks with *gyaku-hanmi katate dori.*

Tori takes a gliding step forwards and then turns 90° outwards. At the same time he brings his hand that is being gripped down to his forward knee. Tori and Uke both sink down into their knees with their upper bodies remaining as upright as possible.

Without pulling at Uke's grip, Tori places his leading leg to the rear and his rear leg forward – at the same time he turns through about 90°. In this way his hand being gripped moves over to the opposite hip side.

Tori takes a gliding step behind Uke and then a step forwards. This step brings the hand being gripped by Uke onto Uke's hip and he pivots round 180° backwards on this axis *(tai-sabaki)*.

This brings Uke off-balance. Uke follows Tori's movement so that he isn't struck on his head by the knee. Tori's hand that is being gripped is brought forwards in the direction of Uke's body so that he can throw him with a further movement of his hips *(tai no henka)*.

Second phase: Tori and Uke each carry out about 50% of the movements. With a step forwards, Uke attacks dynamically with *gyaku-hanmi katate dori*.

Tori takes a gliding step forwards and outwards. Uke grasps hold of Tori's hand – Tori extends this movement outwards and downward by bending his knees down well. His free hand controls the distance to Uke.

Tori eventually controls Uke's head. By virtue of Tori's sideways and downwards movement, Uke is brought off-balance. At the same time Tori takes a step behind Uke.

The same position turned round 180°.

Tori takes a further step behind Uke and using the hand being gripped he fixes this onto Uke's hip as a pivot.

Then Tori turns round about this pivot point 180° backwards *(tai sabaki)* and moves his gripped hand by turning hips further *(tai no hanka)* onto Uke's body. Uke is thus brought off-balance, follows the movement and rolls over forwards.

Third phase: Uke now moves more than Tori. With a step forwards Uke attacks dynamically with a *chudan tsuki*. At the same time, Tori takes a gliding step forwards and outwards. His leading hand is brought onto Uke's arm and slips past Uke's elbow without stopping the attack (but with a possibility of halting Uke).

Tori's rear hand controls the distance to Uke and is then brought past behind Uke's head.

By virtue of his movement to the rear and Uke's attack, Tori is now standing behind Uke and has several possible ways of acting further.

7.5   Application

All basic techniques in Aikido should lead to the internalization of the principles of Aikido (see Chapter 6). The examples of techniques, already given, show once again very clearly that they – particularly in the first and second learning phases – are not designed to function as self-defense techniques against a realistic attack. For this they would be far too slow and the radius of movement far too large. It is more the point that Uke represents a constructive obstacle for Tori, so that he can learn sensibly. Fundamentally, Uke acts neutrally and accepts Tori's moves. These techniques are constructed for Tori's use and not against Uke.

Firstly, once Tori has advanced well in his learning process and has internalized the principles can he begin also to apply the techniques. The Aikido techniques are then modified so that Uke's constructive actions, while being very welcome, are no longer a prerequisite for Tori to be able to execute a movement.

In summary – the learning process in Aikido is represented thus:

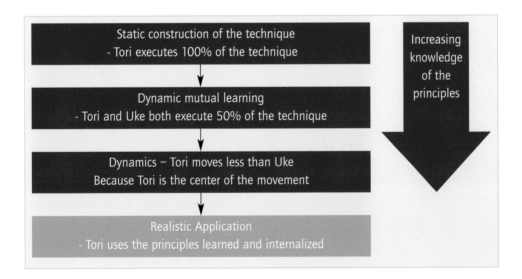

It should be noted once more, that this sequence should only form the background concept for interesting Aikido training. In routine training, differentiations such as these will not be possible always and seem also not very sensible. On the contrary, beginners already partly practice advanced movements, so that they can acquaint themselves with them.

On the other hand, advanced students practice the static construction so that they check their movements.

With reference to the techniques shown in Chapter 7.4, we now show the following examples of application.

mae geri ikkyo omote waza

Uke attacks with *mae geri* (kick at the stomach − see Page 283). The position of the feet for this is *gyaku-hanmi*.

Tori takes a step forwards and at the moment that Uke thinks he can strike Tori, Tori moves past Uke's feet. Tori controls Uke's foot with his leading hand coming down, thus protecting Tori's longitudinal axis guard.

At the same time, Tori's free hand is brought downwards onto Uke's head. This is not intended so much to strike Uke, but rather more aimed at protecting himself and making contact with his hand.

After this has happened, Tori grasps Uke's elbow in his other hand, takes a step forwards and moves his hands in a circular motion downwards. In this way, he begins to control Uke *(ikkyo)*.

Tori now pins Uke's shoulder. He takes a further step forwards and outwards and brings Uke's shoulder down on to the ground. In order to hold Uke firm, Tori kneels down. His inner knee is lying on Uke's shoulder and his outer knee on his wrist. Tori's toes are propped up and his bottom is touching his heels.

mae geri ikkyo ura waza

Uke attacks using a *mae geri* again. Tori takes a gliding step forwards and at the moment that Uke thinks he can strike Tori, Tori moves past Uke's feet. Tori controls Uke's foot at the side. At the same time, Tori's rear hand is brought up towards Uke's head . As described already in *ikkyo omote*, this occurs not intending so much to strike Uke, but rather more aimed at protecting himself and making contact.

At the moment contact is made, Tori pivots round backwards on his leading foot and, with his free hand, grasps hold of Uke's elbow.

Using the grip on Uke's arm Tori brings his shoulder down on to the ground with a circular motion (*ikkyo ura* – see Page 140).

In order to control Uke, Tori kneels down. His inner knee is lying on Uke's shoulder and his outer knee on his wrist. Tori's toes are propped up and his bottom is touching his heels.

The timing is critical in both movements – Tori forces his technique on Uke before Uke has the opportunity to start a second attack.

jodan tsuki soto kaiten nage

Uke attacks with *jodan tsuki* with the feet in the *gyaku-hanmi* position.

At the moment that Uke starts to move forward, Tori also takes a step forwards. His forward hand is protecting his longitudinal axis guard without changing the direction of Uke's strike.

His rear hand controls Uke's longitudinal axis in a flowing movement downwards. Tori glides further forwards with this movement.

Tori is now standing in a better position in relation to Uke and has every possibility to react.

This movement clarifies once again the concept in Aikido that the stronger the attack is, the easier it is for Tori to react, because the power of the attack is not answered by counter-power but by dodging, good timing and correct controlling of the gap between them.

mawashi geri soto kaiten nage

Uke attacks with a *mawashi geri* (roundhouse kick to the side of the head – see Page 285). As soon as Uke starts his kick, Tori takes a step forwards. His rear hand is protecting the side of his head. If the timing is correct then Uke will not hit him.

Tori's other hand is controlling Uke's longitudinal axis with a flowing movement downwards. Tori extends his forward movement by taking a further gliding step forwards.

The starting position turned round 180°.

Tori is now standing in a better position in relation to Uke and has every possibility to react with a movement.

7.6   Working with Priorities

A big challenge in Aikido is to recognize the priorities in the individual movements, take note of them and to overcome the inherent difficulties they bring and, moreover, not to reproduce them every time anew. What is meant by this?

If, for example, Uke attacks with a punch to the head, then the normal reflex is to block it. In time, the *Aikido-ka* learns to control his reflexes so that he doesn't stop the punch but controls it with an Aikido technique. However, dealing with the punch remains the priority in the *Aikido-ka's* actions.

In advanced practice it is possible to take less note of the implication that initially determines how much control has to be exercised over the punch and be able to delay the timing of this so that one is aware of the fact that the punch can be controlled anyway. Instead of this, it is Uke's longitudinal axis that Tori controls first. By delaying this – something that is really important in a movement – Tori opens up opportunities to be quicker and more effective with his techniques.

Another possibility of working with priorities is made clear in the following example of movements:

For simplicity, Uke attacks with *ai-hanmi katate dori*. At the start of practicing Aikido it is a priority for Tori that Uke grasps hold of his wrist (see Page 69).

In time, Tori learns to lift his arm straight up over his head, doing so at exactly the moment that Uke grasps hold of his wrist. So that the attack is made dynamically when training, Uke should have to take a step forward in order to grasp hold of Tori.

With the upward movement of his arm, Tori begins to take a step towards Uke *(irimi)*. Uke's grasping action now loses its importance – Tori has 'solved' this problem himself i.e., the grasping action no longer represents an obstacle that he can't move forward and get into the movement. Uke's elbow is now important, because this poses a potential danger.

Therefore, Tori controls Uke's elbow with his free hand. If Tori succeeds in doing this, then the elbow now loses its importance and he can then get past not only Uke's hand but also his elbow.

It is now possible for Tori to take action against Uke's shoulder or head e.g., with *ikkyo* or *irimi nage*.

Working on the priorities in Aikido fundamentally requires very advanced effort, because the prerequisite for success is to be able to find the correct solutions to certain problems. It is also a big challenge even for advanced students of Aikido, because this means that one has to leave presumed solutions behind and develop oneself further to find the correct ones. The syllable *'do'* in Aikido makes it doubly clear that one has to strive continually to work on oneself and one's movements.

265

7.7   Changing the Rhythm of Movement

All Aikido techniques have a certain rhythm in their movements. When doing the exercises at the beginning, the rhythm is consistent. In particular, Uke has to learn to accept the rhythm set by Tori. For example, he must not suddenly speed up during a movement and 'overtake' Tori. If, at first, Tori's movements are basically very slow, because he has not yet learned to move more rapidly, then Uke's movements must similarly be correspondingly as slow – even if he could be quicker than Tori. Otherwise the learning process for both of them will continually be held up.

If Tori, following his practice, has really understood the sequence of actions in the Aikido techniques, then it will be possible for him to find the correct rhythm. This means that conscious change of rhythm within the sequence of movements is also an important element of the technique. Generally, speeding up a technique serves to get through critical phases of a movement quickly and leave them behind. Similarly, a change of speed can cause Uke to come off-balance. An intentional increase in the rhythm speed can also serve to allow Uke to be pinned down in his movements.

For example, Tori changes the rhythm of movement in an *ushiro ryote dori ikkyo ura* by accelerating when dropping down in his knees thus causing an off-balance situation.

The sudden acceleration in the movement can also serve to throw Uke forwards – as here with *kokyu nage*.

**"The fit describes the capacity of the key,
not of the lock."**

Ernst von Glasersfeld

8   Learning the Role of Uke - ukemi

- What role does Uke play in Aikido?

- What job does Uke carry out in the technique?

- How can Uke attack?

The *Aikido-ka*, who takes on the role of the attacker when exercising is called Uke – when he attacks, he allows *ukemi*. This term stems from the Japanese word *ukeru* that means roughly 'receive'.

Thus, Uke 'receives' the technique from Tori. Even when, at first, this sounds very passive, Uke has some important and active functions in Aikido.

- Because Aikido techniques are constructed so that they only function when being attacked, the rule is – no attack, no Aikido technique. Thus Tori cannot exercise without Uke.

- By virtue of his attack, Uke is the constructive obstacle for Tori and thus the corrective for his movements. For example, Tori will only recognize his mistake of judging the distance by his interplay with Uke.

- The number of possibilities for Uke to move sets the limitation also for Tori's movements. For example, if Uke hasn't learned to be able to fall over forwards (see Chapter 8.4), Tori cannot throw him forwards without accepting the risk of injuring him.

- The quality of Uke's attack determines the quality of Tori's progress in learning. The more accurately Uke attacks, the more he forces Tori to improve his technique.

- By changing over the roles in Aikido, the *Aikido-ka*, whether Uke or Tori, can then use the qualities that he learned as Uke in the role of Tori.

It is no coincidence that the developments in Aikido since its birth (see Chapter 9.4) refer to understanding *ukemi*. In the modern concept of Aikido, Uke is flexible and agile.

He learns to position himself as the attacker and to play an intelligent role in the reciprocal interplay with Tori. His attacks are cohesively and compactly executed.

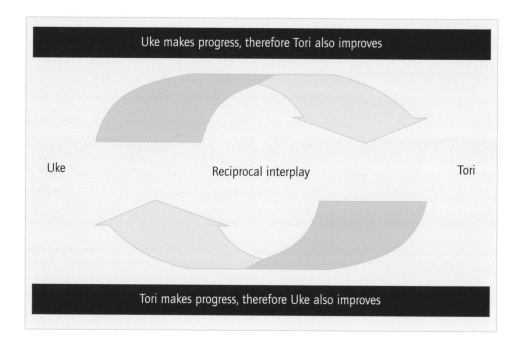

Uke makes progress, therefore Tori also improves

Uke   Reciprocal interplay   Tori

Tori makes progress, therefore Uke also improves

8.1   Getting the Correct Position

It is a priority for Uke, immediately after his attack, to reposition himself in relation to Tori, in order to be able to continue with it and allow Tori to practice his technique. This is, in principle, where there is no differentiation between Aikido and other martial arts or sports. Who can imagine a boxer, who after his initial punch just stands still?

Uke has to keep his positioning such that he follows the Aikido principle of having his feet, one behind the other, in a line. He also tries to keep the angle of his position so that he controls Tori with its angle. When moving, Uke avoids having to cross over his feet or legs. Rather, he corrects his distance first of all by always taking a gliding step.

The following example of movements should illustrate this point:

Uke grasps hold of Tori's jacket at shoulder height *(kata dori)*. Tori dodges this attack just prior to Uke gripping. To do this he takes a step forwards and outwards and pivots round backwards on his leading foot *(tai-sabaki)*.

Uke adjusts his position in relation to Tori by taking a step forwards and extending this into a gliding step.

Uke now adopts a position so that using his grip he can control the angle in which he is standing to Tori.

He can use the grip to get round behind Tori and bring him off-balance.

Maintaining Contact

After advanced training, Uke concentrates on not only continuing with his attack, but also on maintaining contact with Tori. This means that Uke doesn't necessarily have to grasp him but rather, he maintains a point of contact – usually the hands or arms – to carry on controlling him. They 'stick together' – so to speak – as soon as they touch. Therefore, Uke and Tori have a joint interest in making contact with each other, so that Uke carries on sensibly with his attack and Tori can defend himself without causing any unnecessary injury to Uke.

The correct feeling for making contact can be trained for outside the actual technique exercises.

First exercise: Uke and Tori are standing diagonally opposite each other. The hands are crossed over with the back of them pointing to each other. The hands 'stick' together at the point of contact. Using horizontally executed, circular motions, each tries alternately to touch the other's head.

Second exercise: Uke and Tori are standing in the same starting position as before – but, now, at such a distance from each other so that, without taking a further step, they will not be able to reach each other. Tori leads in making contact with Uke, who tries to maintain the distance and the contact.

Third exercise: Uke's and Tori's palms are touching each other ('sticking together'). The hand that is uppermost is pointing towards the opponent's neck. The hand that is underneath controls the pressure by keeping contact with the upper hand. Uke can now be steered by the movement of the upper hand.

8.2   Working with Agreements

As discussed several times already (see Chapter 7), to learn Aikido, Tori and Uke require to have clear pre-agreed actions between themselves. This is comparable to the fact that two people generally must speak the same language in order to have a conversation. Basically there are pre-agreed actions like these in all the martial arts. This starts with simple things like the agreement to be at the dojo at a laid down time, having to wear a *gi* (exercise uniform) etc.

In Aikido, moreover, the pre-arranged actions mean that Uke and Tori can constructively practice together. Especially for Uke, this means, for example, that he must position himself in a particular way (see Chapter 8.1) and by remaining in an attacking posture, give Tori the opportunity to execute the technique. In *tenkan ho* (see Chapter 2.4) there is, for example, the pre-arrangement that Uke, using his grip, allows Tori to feel the point of contact. In this exercise, nothing would keep him from simply letting go. Pre-arranged actions in Aikido similarly follow the logic of any martial art: Uke maintains his intention of attacking or maintains contact with Tori in order also to be able to keep his position under control.

The aim in Tori's learning process is for him to be gradually less dependent on the pre-arranged actions and then still be able to execute the techniques even if Uke doesn't keep to the agreements. As already often said, this calls for a great deal of prowess from Tori and one in which he can bring in and make use of the principles of Aikido successfully.

Depending on the Aikido style being used (see Chapter 9.4) and the concept connected with it, there can be, moreover, several different pre-arranged actions. Within the framework of the individual different styles, the pre-arranged actions are consistent with that style. However, the question comes in considering the concept which kind of pre-arranged action brings what development perspectives with it. For this there are many quite different, possible answers.

8.3   Attacking Correctly

A great number of different forms of attack are practiced in Aikido – grasping from the front, behind, punching or striking with the edge of the hand or fist and, of course, kicking. The idea behind this is to learn as broad a spectrum of movements as possible. This way, the *Aikido-ka* learns to stick to the principles of Aikido in quite differing situations and to be able to use them.

With reference to the attacks in Aikido, sometimes misunderstandings crop up that they are not realistic. Firstly, we can only say that this question is of no interest to martial arts. It poses rather the following questions: What challenges and topics do the different attacks in Aikido bring to the person practicing them? And, are the results of this learning process then transferable to any form of realistic attack? On a basic conceptual level, this second question can be answered with a clear "Yes!" Whether a person is really able to defend himself using Aikido is reliant on that person, the situation and the opponent and not on Aikido itself. One would not accuse a boxer who has been knocked out that boxing itself doesn't function.

The following standard forms of attack are generally practiced in Aikido – they can also, of course, be combined. The details of the footwork must be taken as orientation aids in order to maintain a degree of plausibility in the attack. In the end, Uke can attack just as he wishes. So that Uke and Tori can learn the basic techniques in Aikido, both rely on pre-arranged positions of the feet (see Chapter 2.1).

ai-hanmi katate dori

This form of attack is more to do with a learning form, allowing better understanding of the Aikido techniques, rather than a real form of attack. This is because Uke, in using a grasping action, cannot control Tori at the angle at which they stand together.

Uke grasps Tori's wrist diagonally (*te* = wrist, *dori* = grasp) – both are standing with their same side of the body (also same foot) leading (*ai-hanmi* = same position) – either left side forward or right side forward. Tori's hand can also be twisted round so that the thumb is downward (see Page 69).

gyaku-hanmi katate dori

Uke grasps hold of Tori's wrist on the mirror-image side (*gyaku* = not the same/opposite). For this, Uke's right-hand side leads and for Tori his left-hand side leads or vice versa. Uke is not standing directly frontally on to Tori, but using the grip, he can control the angle at which he stands to Tori.

kata dori

Uke grasps hold of Tori's jacket at shoulder height (*kata* = shoulder). As in the *gyaku-hanmi katate dori*, he can control the angle at which he stands to Tori as Uke is not standing directly frontally on to Tori.

muna dori

Uke grasps hold of Tori's lapel at chest height. The feet can be in either a diagonal or mirror-image position.

katate ryote dori

Uke grasps hold of one of Tori's arms or wrists *(katate)* in both hands *(ryote)*. Normally the first contact is made between the edges of the two hands with the feet positioned diagonally.

Uke brings Tori's arm downwards and begins to grip with both hands.

At the same time, he changes over to a mirror-image position with his feet, so that he can control the angle to Tori.

The *katate ryote dori* attack is also called *morote dori*.

kata dori men uchi

Uke grasps hold of Tori's jacket at shoulder height *(kata dori)*.

He uses this grip and the angle at which he is standing to Tori to control him and bring him forward off-balance. He is then standing behind Tori's back and can use his free hand to strike Tori's neck *(men uchi)*.

If Uke can execute this attack completely, then it is too late to employ an Aikido technique. Therefore, Tori anticipates Uke's movement and, at the moment that Uke grasps hold of the jacket at shoulder height, he takes a gliding step forwards and outwards. At the same time, he brings his leading hand upwards in the direction of Uke's head.

ryote dori

Uke grasps hold of both of Tori's wrists *(ryote)* with his feet in the mirror-image position. If Uke's left leg is forward then his left hand is lower. The other hand grasps over the first so that the position is firm. Using the grip, Uke controls the angle to Tori.

ryo hiji dori

Uke grasps both *(ryo)* of Tori's elbows *(hiji)*. The feet are placed in the diagonal position.

ryo kata dori

Uke grasps hold of Tori's shoulders by the jacket. The feet are placed in the diagonal position.

shomen uchi

Uke strikes *(uchi)* downward onto Tori's head *(men)* with the edge of his hand. Uke swings his hand up along his longitudinal axis ready to hit downwards. Uke takes a step forwards and already begins with the forward movement to strike downward so that Tori cannot stop him with his forward leading hand.

At the moment that Uke hits Tori, the feet are in the diagonal position. In order to reach Tori, Uke can also take a gliding step forward, in which case the movement begins right from the diagonal starting position.

yokomen uchi

Uke strikes downwards with a diagonal movement onto the side (*yoko* = side) of Tori's head with the edge of his hand. Uke swings his hand up along his longitudinal axis over his head ready to hit downwards. Uke takes a step forwards and already begins with the forward movement to strike downward so that Tori cannot stop him with his forward leading hand.

At the moment that Uke hits Tori, the feet are in the mirror-image position. In order to reach Tori, Uke can also take a gliding step forward, in which case the movement begins right from the mirror-image starting position.

men uchi

Uke punches towards Tori's face. Contrary to *jodan tsuki* (see below) he doesn't ball his hand into a fist. The fingers are only bent loosely into the palm. The idea behind this attack is that at the last moment the fist is bunched up or the hand grasps at Uke's neck or hair. This kind of attack serves to give Uke a feeling for a quick and relaxed move forward of his hand. The feet are placed in the diagonal position.

jodan tsuki

Uke punches towards Tori's face. The feet are placed either in the diagonal position or in a mirror-image position.

The fingers are closed together with the thumb outside and the back of the hand and the lower arm form a line with each other.

Uke uses the knuckles of the fore and

middle finger to strike with. At the moment of striking, the wrist can be twisted over towards the side where the thumb is.

chudan tsuki

Uke punches with his fist towards Tori's stomach or solar plexus. The feet are placed either in the diagonal position or in a mirror-image position.

In all the martial arts, there are three target areas of the body to aim punches or kicks at:

- *jodan:* Upper area – i.e., head and neck.
- *chudan:* Middle area – i.e., abdomen (stomach) and solar plexus.
- *gedan:* Lower area – i.e., from the belt line downwards.

mae geri

Uke kicks *(geri)* directly at Tori's stomach. For this, Uke, in a first phase lifts his knee up sharply. The feet are placed either in the diagonal position or in a mirror-image position.

By rapidly kicking his foot out forward, Uke hits with the ball of his foot.

mae geri – irimi

mawashi geri

Uke kicks out at the side of Tori's head. For this, Uke, in a first phase lifts his knee up sharply. The feet are placed either in the diagonal position or in a mirror-image position.

Then, he kicks with the back of the foot sideways at Tori's head.

ushiro ryote dori

In Aikido, attacks from the rear *(ushiro)* always start from the front – see the following logic: If Uke is behind Tori there are two possibilities. Either, Tori notices Uke and turns round and then both of them are standing directly opposite each other, or, Tori doesn't notice Uke. In this case he doesn't have any further chance, theoretically, to sensibly meet an attack.

Therefore, in spite of this, how does Uke get behind Tori? In the first moment contact is made between the edges of their hands touching each other diagonally.

Uke brings Tori's arm downwards and grasps hold of the wrist. Tori leaves the line of attack to one side and begins to move forwards. The angle between Uke and Tori is now such that Uke can get round behind Tori.

So that Uke can control Tori, he grasps hold of the other wrist. As he does this he grasps hold so that his thumbs are upwards.

ushiro ryo hiji dori

The movement starts as in the *ushiro ryote dori*, however, Uke and Tori are standing close together at the beginning, so that Uke can control Tori's elbows *(hiji)*.

Tori dodges again outwards and forwards so that Uke gets round behind him.

Uke's grip prevents Tori from turning round.

ushiro ryo kata dori

The movement starts as in the *ushiro ryote dori*, however, the distance between Uke and Tori is now even less so that Uke can grasp hold of Tori's jacket by the shoulders.

Tori dodges outwards and forwards so that Uke gets round behind him.

Uke's grip prevents Tori from turning round.

ushiro katate dori kubi shime

As in the *ushiro ryote dori*, Uke brings Tori's arm downwards and grasps hold of the wrist. By virtue of Tori's movement outwards and forwards, Uke can get round behind Tori's back.

Uke grasps round and takes hold of Tori's lapel and can start doing a strangle lock.

The same position seen from the other side (180°).

ushiro eri dori

As in the *ushiro ryote dori*, Uke brings Tori's arm downwards and grasps hold of the wrist. By virtue of Tori's movement outwards and forwards, Uke can get round behind Tori's back.

Using his free hand, Uke now grasps hold of Tori's collar. He can also let go of his grip on Tori's wrist and use this hand to grasp the collar.

8.4   Rolling and Falling (Breakfalls)

So that Uke can take part in the Aikido throws sensibly, he has to learn to be able to do rolls and falls. Only once Uke has mastered the falling movements, and thus minimize the risk of injury, can Tori then carry out his throwing actions resolutely. This point makes it clear again that Uke and Tori are reliant on each other for their development.

Rolling Over Backward - ushiro ukemi

This basic falling movement is done by rolling from the kneeling position, over on to the bottom and then on to the back.

The *Aikido-ka* is standing in the starting position.

He kneels down on the rear knee. The instep of the foot lies flat on the ground.

He can now roll over on his bottom and back so that the head doesn't touch the ground. The legs are stretched out and the feet are brought together.

During the rollover backwards, first of all, the palm of the one hand slaps the ground (on the side where Uke was kneeling).

Then the other hand slaps the ground. It's now possible to stand up again in the reverse order (kneeling then starting position).

Slapping the ground with the hands serves to dissipate the energy of the falling movement. This allows Uke to fall down safely even when Tori does a powerful throw. When starting Aikido training, the backward roll can be practiced straight from the kneeling position.

Variation

In some throws (e.g., *shiho nage*) it is necessary to continue dissipating the energy of the movement by making an additional move sideways.

After rolling over backwards, the legs are crossed over.

The back does not stay flat on the mat. Uke keeps looking at Tori. Uke stands up again in the reverse order.

Rolling Over Forward - mae ukemi

From some throws (e.g., *kaiten nage, ude kime nage*), it is only possible to roll over forward.

Uke rolls forward over his forward arm. He twists the edge of the hand outwards to make sure the arm is rounded.

During the fall, it is important that the arm is kept stable and is not bent.

Uke can now roll over the shoulder, his back and bottom. During the whole of the rollover movement the head does not touch the floor.

During the rollover movement, the palm of the hand slaps the ground. As in rolling over backward, slapping the ground helps to dissipate the energy of the movement. This keeps the rollover compact. At the same time, this is a preparatory exercise for falling over forward.

Falling over backward is identical to falling over forward – just simply done in the opposite direction. Uke kneels down first of all and then rolls over his bottom and his back. Then he rolls onto the side where his knee was positioned and over onto his shoulder. His arm is also positioned on this side, just like falling over forward. This allows him to 'roll' over his arm.

Falling Forward – High Breakfall

A further form of falling over forward is the high breakfall. Uke falls forward when Tori's throwing action is done so quickly that Uke cannot follow the movement with a falling over forward or a falling over backward action. In other words, Tori, by virtue of the speed of his action, the angle he is at to Uke and his determined throw, causes Uke to fall forward with a breakfall.

The sequence of this falling movement is identical to falling over forward – this time, however, the fall occurs, so that the axis of rotation is not carried out by rolling on the floor.

In order for the *Aikido-ka* to learn to fall or roll safely, it seems sensible to practice the sequence first of all on his own (i.e., without the throwing action). For example, a good way is to fall down over your partner. The axis of rotation then takes place over your partner's back.

This should not occur with too much pressure being applied to the partner's back. Rather, the rotation should come from your own impulse over the obstacle. The free hand – used to do the slapping motion onto the mat – leads well in front of the body and the legs.

This way the energy is dissipated and it is possible to stand up again straight away.

The same movement done following a *shiho nage* throw: The axis of rotation is done about Uke's wrist. The free arm is first in touching the mat – i.e., before the body does.

8.5   Advanced Falling Techniques

Mae ukemi and *ushiro ukemi* are the basic falling techniques in Aikido. Uke's repertoire is now increased by adding two advanced falling techniques.

Handstand Fall

The so-called handstand fall comes with several technique variations – e.g., direct forms of *ikkyo omote* – or for use as an alternative to *mae ukemi* when there isn't sufficient room available for rolling movements.

The movement can be practiced alone in the following way: Both hands are placed on the ground relatively close to the feet. The feet are then brought rapidly up into the air with a dynamic motion.

You can now roll down in a controlled manner on to the torso and the stomach.

As you do this, you turn your head to one side.

Here, we show the same movement as done in the *hanmi handachi ai-hanmi katate dori ikkyo omote* technique: Following a step forward, Uke grasps hold of Tori's wrist. Tori places his forward knee to one side and, in this way dodges sideways.

With his free hand, Tori grasps hold of Uke's elbow.

Using his grip on Uke's arm, Tori now brings Uke's shoulder down on to the ground. Uke sweeps his leading leg away with his rear leg, supports himself on the ground with his free hand and kicks his feet up into the air. This way he can deal sensibly with Tori's holding technique without landing uncomfortably on the ground.

Falling Like a Leaf

In order to fall like a leaf, the *Aikido-ka* brings his hips forward in a dynamic movement and kicks his legs up in the air.

Slapping the ground occurs first with one hand. You then roll down over the arm and the shoulder girdle until the other arm is near the ground.

Finally, you can do a controlled roll over the back. The head does not touch the mat.

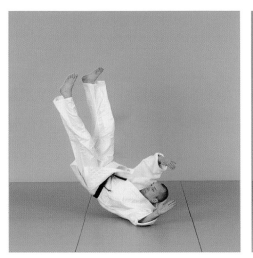

8.6   Ukemi as a Part of the Technique

At the end of this chapter, we want to delve further into three other sequences of movements that crop up in the framework of the basic techniques in Aikido and of particular interest.

irimi nage

As always in *ukemi*, it is the same in *irimi nage* i.e., that Uke accepts the movement but then repositions himself in relation to Tori. As a general rule, Uke will be brought off-balance with *irimi nage*.

Using his leading foot, he adjusts his position and his inside hand is placed on the ground to control the imbalance. His rear leg is moved upwards as a counter-balance to his leading hand. He then takes a step forwards. So that Uke can control Tori's arm he takes yet a further step forwards towards the arm.

With his repositioning, Uke can stay close to the center of the movement and is not spun outwards by the centrifugal force. Thus it is still possible for him to retain control over the movement.

If Tori brings the action down lower or brings Uke further off-balance, then Uke can do a controlled landing on his inside knee and his lower arm.

In this position, Uke can still see Tori as well as be able to take a move in any direction. Uke now brings his rear foot forwards and begins to stand up. He then takes a further step towards Tori's arm in order to control it. Throughout this sequence of movements, Uke should try to remain always relaxed but compact.

Holding Techniques

In all holding techniques, Uke ends up lying on the ground. In the *omote* movement, he brings his forward knee and the free hand on to the ground. He then lets Tori lay him on the ground.

Uke tries to keep his shoulder relaxed. If Tori was to apply a lot of pressure on Uke's arm, Uke could give way immediately because his shoulder was relaxed.

In *ura* movements, Uke follows up with his inside foot and then places his inside knee down on to the ground.

The outer hand follows in order to control the downward movement.

As in *omote*, at the same time Uke keeps his shoulder and his arm as relaxed as possible in order to give into Tori's movement.

ikkyo omote waza

In the main holding technique in Aikido – *ikkyo* – in the basic form, it is Uke's job to do the following:

After his *shomen uchi* attack, Uke (left) is controlling e.g., Tori's uppermost hand, so that he is not struck by it himself.

As Tori is, in addition, controlling Uke's elbow, Uke has to keep his arm loose and bent inwards.

Detail of the hand position

Uke now moves with a gliding step further in Tori's direction. Uke has now achieved the distance so that he can continue his attack with his free hand.

The challenge for Tori's is to close up his own position at the same moment, so not to be struck, and then control Uke (see Chapter 5.3).

8.7   Using Your Body Weight

In Aikido, Uke first of all, learns how to attack, punch etc., correctly – initially in a static position and then working up to dynamic actions. Eventually, he learns how to position himself and thus be able to react to Tori's movements. As he progresses to a higher level, Uke also learns to be relaxed in his movements but still remain compact. Only by doing all these things, can Uke reach a sufficiently high level of prowess to be able to follow Tori's movements and keep the risk of injury to a minimum.

Along with this development comes the idea that Uke can become an interesting opponent for Tori, when he uses his body weight in the movement, for example in *irimi nage* or *ikkyo*. Ideally, he is relaxed (not to be confused with slackness) and able to react, remain compact and heavy (not to be confused with his clumsiness). In the training sessions, this creates an interesting form of cooperation, because Tori has to make efforts to bring Uke off-balance. When making these efforts, Tori can soon find out if he is correctly positioned and whether he is stable enough and is lowering his body well enough. At the same time, Uke learns the qualities that he would need likewise when acting as Tori, namely to be relaxed and compact.

As a résumé of Chapter 8, Uke's qualities in Aikido can be described as follows:

- Attack correctly.

- React to Tori's movements appropriately and sensibly.

- Be able to fall safely.

- Remain compact and relaxed in his movements.

- Gradually be able to use his body weight.

"All war is deception."

Sun Tzu

9 Further Information

- How do you warm up?

- What are *dan* and *kyu* grades?

- Where do you find more information?

This Chapter is all about more information that would be interesting for the *Aikido-ka* and a good way to conclude this book away from the techniques and basic concepts of Aikido, illustrated and covered in the previous chapters.

9.1 Correct Warm-up

Every Aikido session usually begins with a warm-up phase. Because the Aikido techniques are all carried out within the normal radius of body movement, there is no requirement for extreme physical flexibility. In spite of this, the value and purpose of the warm-up phase should be clear to students and instructors and they also should posses a basic knowledge about the physiological processes.

Physiological Changes in Warm-ups

By doing warm-ups, first of all the temperature of the body rises. The optimum temperature to deal with the stresses of sport lies between 38.5° and 39° C. You can feel whether your body is ready for the movements or is 'still cold', even without the use of a thermometer. Besides the rise in temperature, there are numerous other physiological changes taking place. Warm-ups affect the cardiovascular system, the muscles, the joints, the nerves and even the state of mind. We take a closer look at the influence these play in the following paragraphs.

The whole of the cardiovascular system adapts to the coming challenges of activity by a change in breathing and heart rate. The metabolic rate of the body is increased and the flow of blood to the muscles is increased by six-fold more than before the activity. The supply of oxygen to the muscles is improved and this results in better efficiency in getting them to produce more powerful, quicker and enduring muscle tension and relaxation. Additionally, wastes from the production of energy – carbon dioxide and lactic acid – are got rid of. This prevents a build up of lactic acid in the cells that causes rapid muscle fatigue.

A further influence on the muscle system through the warm-up is quite obvious for many *Aikido-ka*. The muscles become noticeably looser. This is the result of a reduction in the resistance between the muscle fibers as well as the increased ability to tense and relax the muscle. These changes lead to a distinct decrease in the vulnerability to injury. For example, if an antagonist muscle of a powerful, quickly tensed muscle can be easily relaxed then it will be less liable to ripping. Besides this, a movement will occur economically and quickly when only the muscle connected to that movement is tensed. Protection, by virtue of having relaxed muscles is made also clear with another example. If an arm is loose then the direction of a lever or throw can be sensed better and followed, thus any injury avoided.

Appropriate warm-ups can reduce the risk of injury in the area of the so-called 'passive' parts of the body (bones, joints and ligaments). In the course of the warm-up, the joint cartilages thicken. This allows external forces to be cushioned better. In Aikido, this is very important, because there are techniques that are carried out using extremely angular positions of the joints or that exert extreme pressure on the joints (e.g., as in *suwari waza* or *nikkyo ura*).

The most influential change for Aikido that occurs in the warm-up is, however, the changes in the function of the nervous system. Higher temperature increases the speed at which nerve impulses are transmitted. Thus, the body temperature influences the ability to react and this is, of course, crucial in an attack such as *jodan tsuki*. However, it is not only the speed of the nerve impulse that is speeded up by warming up, the sensitive stimulation of the nerves is also increased. Sensory perception, such as touch or depth perception, muscle tension and body movement (called proprioception - the ability to sense the position and location and orientation and movement of the body and its parts), is optimized. This is the best prerequisite for good feelings of the body and its movements. You can get a better idea of your own center of balance as well as that of your partner.

An additional important effect of the warm-up is to get into the mood for the upcoming challenge. Repetition or the action of carrying out similar exercises transmits the signal: Let's go! This leads to an activation of the mental state of mind that is accompanied by an increased ability to concentrate. Thus the *Aikido-ka* is brought right up to the mark, so to speak.

A tip on the side for all those who suffer from aches of the muscles: Although warm-ups are beneficial, unfortunately, muscle aches (tiny tears in the fibers of the muscle) are not prevented by doing them. Training more often and drinking cherry juice help this!

At a glance, here, once again are the benefits of warm-ups:

• Lower chance of getting injured.

• Better performance and awareness of the body.

• Less build up of lactic acid in the muscle system.

• Getting into the right mood and better concentration.

Warming Up in Aikido

The exercises described in the following paragraphs are examples for a possible warm-up for Aikido and are in no way to be understood as mandatory. The style of Aikido range from meditative, slow movements to sportingly, dynamic forms of workout. Since the warm-up should be adapted to the content of the upcoming instruction session, it must just be as varied. At best, account should be taken of the age and the physical condition of the *Aikido-ka*, as well as the time of day and the ambient temperature of the training location.

Firstly, an increase in the temperature of the working muscles should be strived for in the general part of the warm-up training. For this, as many of the larger muscles as possible should be brought into play. This should be done with a low to medium intensity. Possible exercises for this are hopping on the spot or doing varied running movements.

This can be followed up by doing exercises to mobilize the muscles and joints. Examples for this are doing exercises to loosen the joints such as circling the arms, shoulders and hips etc. From an anatomical point of view, some traditional exercises such as circling the knees and head are not recommended, because the knee only has a 10° freedom of movement sideways and the connection between the head and the trunk is not a ball joint! As an alternative, do knee bends and stretches. The head can be rolled forward and backwards and moved left and right.

After this, you should do stretching exercises of the various muscle groups (see below).

Warning: Stretching exercises should not be carried out with sudden, jerky movements or be painful. There is a variety of possible stretching exercises – for Aikido, examples of the relevant methods are:

- Static Stretching Exercises (here, we abbreviate this to 'SSE' [1]).

- Dynamic Stretching Exercises (here, we abbreviate this to 'DSE' [1]).

- Muscle Tension-Relaxation (PMR – Progressive Muscle Relaxation)

In SSE, each stretching position is adopted and held for a few seconds. This method of stretching is easily controllable and can therefore be used by everyone. In this connection, although the capability of the muscle to tension rapidly and powerfully is decreased with this, specific sports exercises that follow can balance out this effect.

Because Aikido is characterized by dynamic movements, dynamic stretching exercises (DSE) are particularly, very suitable. For this, you carry out various stretching exercises in a springy and bouncy manner and as far as your movements will allow. Following any injury, this type of stretching exercise should be used with great care.

In exercises for PMR, first of all the muscle system is tensed firmly, then relaxed and tensed again. This method of stretching exercise gives you the greatest gain in movement and flexibility of all the methods described here. The muscle system is warmed up and strengthened. Because each of the methods cannot be used for every stretching exercise, in the following examples we have added the suitability of the methods in brackets at the end of the individual exercise.

---

[1]   The abbreviation is not an official one, but used for ease in this book to indicate usage in the description of later exercises. PMR is an official abbreviation.

First Part: Neck, Chest and Lumbar Vertebra of the Backbone

The legs are crossed over in the standing position and the trunk pushed over to the same side of the leading leg position without twisting the upper body. At the same time, the arms are propped up on the hips. The trunk muscles on the side are stretched as well as strengthened in this exercise (SSE, DSE).

Second Part: Shoulder Joints and Shoulder Girdle

Standing with legs shoulder-width apart and knees slightly bent, bring the arms bent up behind the head. At the same time the elbows are at shoulder level and are actively pushed to the rear. The shoulder muscles, but also the stomach and rib muscles, are stretched in this exercise. The shoulder girdle muscle group will also be strengthened (static but active stretching position).

Third Part: Hip and Knee Joints

With one knee bent and the other leg stretched out (groin stretch), your weight is placed over the bent knee. The foot of the outstretched leg is placed flat on the ground and the toes face forward. This exercise stretches those muscles that pull the outstretched leg to the body (adductor muscle). In order to stretch various parts of the muscle, the outstretched leg can be rotated outwards (SSE, DSE, PMR).

Adopt a low down knees bent squatting position. The knees point in the same direction as the toes. The stretching action is reinforced by using the elbows on the inside of the knees. This exercise serves to stretch the adductor muscles as well as a part of the calf muscles (SSE, PMR).

Sit with one leg stretched out and the other leg crossed over it. The foot of that leg is placed down by the knee of the other leg. The elbow on the side of the outstretched leg aids with the stretching rotation while the other arm props the body up. The abductor muscle and the buttock muscle group are stretched in thus exercise (SSE, DSE, PMR).

Adopting a lunging step position with one leg, bring the weight of the body over it and bring the opposite arm out forward. The rear leg is bent at the knee. By pushing the hips forward the front of the thigh of the rear leg is stretched. This stretching exercise adjusts for the invigoration of the thigh muscle in Aikido and also aids in preventing a wrong position of the pelvis and spinal cord (SSE, DSE).

Fourth Part: Ankle Joints

As before, adopt a lunging step position with one leg and bring the weight of the body over it. The rear leg is now kept stretched straight. The hands are placed on the hips. It is important that the heel of the stretched leg is flat on the ground. This exercise stretches the calf muscles (SSE, DSE, PMR).

The transition between the final warm-up phase performing sports exercises and the main part of the instruction session can be done, flowing from one to the other. Here, preparatory exercises such as *tenkan* or *tai-sabaki* for example (see Chapter 2) as well as rolls and falling exercises (see Chapter 8.4) can be included.

At the beginning of the main part of the instructional session, the techniques should be done, first of all, with a low intensity. Furthermore, exercises using extremely angular positions of the body – for example as in *suwari waza* - should be avoided, because the warming effect on the joints described above only begins properly after at least 20 minutes. Ideal exercises for the beginning of the session are those techniques where the *Aikido-ka* has to move about a lot (e.g., *uchi kaiten nage*) or where they can be carried out without a lot of explanation and sitting around with the inherent cooling off happening.

Although this chapter is about warming UP, in conclusion just a few words about cooling OFF. Where the timing of a session allows it, a cooling off phase should be built in for the last few minutes. This aids the recovery process and the rapid return to coping with further pressure, not only in Aikido but also in everyday routine. The best way is to reduce the intensity of the last few techniques so that the metabolism of the muscles can become normalized. Only after this can further stretching exercises benefit the regeneration process and also contribute to a relaxed state of mind.

9.2   Equipment, Exercise Area and Etiquette

A white *Judo* uniform *(keiko-gi)* must be worn for Aikido training. These are available in various sizes, quality and price range. Thin *Karate* uniforms are not very practical, because in Aikido attacks are carried out where the jacket has to be pulled.

As a general rule, a white belt is worn with the *keiko-gi* until one has gained the first *dan* – the color of this belt is then black (see Chapter 9.3).

In addition to the *keiko-gi*, in Aikido, a Japanese traditional pair of pants (culottes) – called *hakama* – is worn. These are either black or blue and similarly are available in different qualities and prices. Just when the *hakama* is worn is dependent on the grade held and is dealt with differently from club to club and school to school.

gi

hakama

Because weapons are used to practice with in Aikido, the *Aikido-ka* needs to have a wooden staff *(jo)*, a wooden sword *(bokken)* and a wooden knife *(tanto)* – at least if he is going to take a serious interest in Aikido. There are also various different kinds of these and they come in different prices. Very often, these exercise weapons are also available on loan from your *dojo* (see next page).

jo – wooden staff

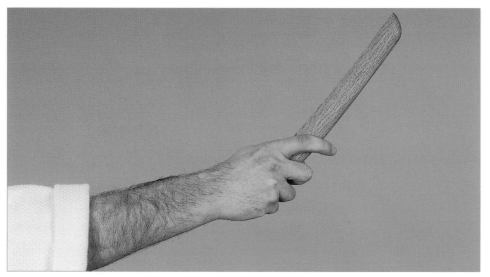

tanto – (wooden) knife

In many *dojos*, the shoes must be removed before entering. So that you can move around comfortably in the training area, you need to have sandals or so-called *zori* (made of Japanese rice straw).

The word *dojo* is made up from *'do'* (having the same meaning as in Aikido) and *'jo'* i.e., the place where something takes place. This can be translated literally as "The place where the 'way' is practiced". An Aikido *dojo* is a room fitted with *Judo* mats. You will usually always find a portrait hanging of the founder of Aikido – Morihei Ueshiba – and there will perhaps be a *kamiza* hanging bearing an Aikido calligraphy.

A *dojo*, however, is more than a training hall. Irrespective of the room layout, what sets a *dojo* apart from other things, is that the people practicing in it do so with respect to others and try to follow the way that is laid down by Aikido in an earnest manner. This attitude is expressed in a particular kind of etiquette – the Japanese expression is *reigi* (*rei* = politeness, greeting).

Whenever the *Aikido-ka* enters the *dojo*, he should bow to the portrait of Morihei Ueshiba and also bow when he leaves it.

The Aikido lesson always begins and ends by the instructors and the students first bowing before the portrait of the founder of Aikido and then bowing to each other.

This has nothing to do with worship or subjugation. The bow is an expression of mutual respect and politeness. After all, you wouldn't be able to practice Aikido if Morihei Ueshiba had not existed.

To bow, you bring your hands together forward, the back remains straight and your bottom is resting on your heels.

The standing bow:

At the beginning and at the end of the instruction or in short pauses from training, you sit down on your heels *(seiza)*. In this position, the mentality in the *dojo* is also expressed. The *Aikido-ka* can act immediately, for example stand up or move into a *shikko* position (see Chapter 2.9), and remain attentive and concentrated.

The shoulders are held relaxed and the upper body is held up straight. The hands hang loosely down on the thighs.

9.3   The Grading System

In all traditional martial arts it is possible to take grading tests – generally these are optional. A distinction is made between *kyu* and *dan* grades. One begins with the kyu grades. Normally in Aikido you begin with the Fifth *kyu* and these then count backwards the higher grade you achieve.

The purpose of the *kyu* grading tests is to get you to work with the names of the Aikido techniques, gradually learn them and understand the systematic build up of Aikido. Getting to terms, not only physically but also intellectually, with Aikido increases the general success in learning, because it will be possible, for example, to distinguish between basic and advanced techniques and employ variations or applications. By taking the grading tests, the *Aikido-ka* will also be able to judge better just where he stands with his progress and what he necessarily has to practice next (see Chapter 7).

If the *Aikido-ka* has graduated in the grading test for the 1st *kyu*, then he should know and be able to carry out all the basic techniques.

It will now be possible to take the grading test for the 1st *dan* after which he is allowed to wear the black belt. This should not be confused with a mastership grade in Aikido. The Japanese character for *shodan* (the 1st *dan*) has more a meaning of "at the beginning". Put bluntly, one is just at the beginning of actual Aikido training, as the only thing known yet is the basic techniques.

From now on, the numbers count logically upwards. For the 2nd, 3rd and 4th dan, the *Aikido-ka* has to improve his techniques, get more into working them up and internalize the principles. At the same time he must more or less keep strictly to the laid down basic techniques *(kata)*, and work on and with them. Dependent on the physical constitution of the person practicing and his keenness, Uke learns also to attack with force and punch well – on the other side, Tori learns how to stop these attacks or cushion and control them with his techniques. Similarly, Tori practices to overcome Uke with his techniques and move him even when, for example Uke tries to block the techniques. The *Aikido-ka* can get to terms first of all in this non-competitive interplay and achieve the necessary self-assuredness for a martial art by reaching a higher stage.

The last grading test that can be taken by the *Aikido-ka* is generally that of the 4th *dan* – higher grades are awarded.

With the 4th and 5th *dan* in Aikido, you begin to reach the stage of independent development and a mastership class, since now the *Aikido-ka* has not only mastered the techniques, but, after many years of practice he understands the principles and has internalized them as far as possible.

As an example of a simple *kyu* grading test, here we show the grading test program for the *hombu dojo* in Tokyo (see Page 335). Many organizations, in the meanwhile, have developed their own standards.

The course of events in a grading test in Aikido, is generally as follows: The candidate is given the name of an attack and technique and he has to execute this with his Uke several times. In the execution, the candidate has to be careful not only to show a correct technical sequence of movements, but also to give a good demonstration of the technique. To a certain degree, this, of course is dependent on the grade being strived for. This includes, for example:

- To remain stable at the end of each throwing movement.
- To conclude each holding technique correctly (i.e., with a short pause).
- For kneeling techniques (*suwari* or *hanmi handachi waza*) not touch the mat with the hands.

HOMBU DOJO GRADING SYSTEM

	ikkyo	nikkyo	sankyo	yonkyo	gokyo	shiho nage
5. kyu	shomen uchi					gyaku-hanmi katate dori
4. kyu	shomen uchi	gyaku-hanmi katate dori				yokomen uchi
3. kyu	shomen uchi (suwari & tachi waza)					ryote dori yokomen uchi
2. kyu	shomen uchi (suwari & tachi waza) kata dori (suwari & tachi waza)					gyaku-hanmi katate dori (hanmi handachi)
1. kyu	shomen uchi (suwari & tachi waza) yokomen uchi (suwari & tachi waza) kata dori (suwari & tachi waza) ushiro ryote dori			yokomen uchi		gyaku-hanmi katate dori ryote dori (hanmi handachi & tachi waza)

irimi nage	kote geashi	kaiten nage	tenchi nage	jiyu waza	kokyu ho
shomen uchi					suwari waza
shomen uchi					suwari waza
shomen uchi chudan tsuki			ryote dori		suwari waza
shomen uchi chudan tsuki gyaku-hanmi katate dori	gyaku-hanmi katate dori		ryote dori	gyaku-hanmi katate dori	suwari waza
shomen uchi chudan tsuki gyaku-hanmi katate dori			ryote dori	gyaku-hanmi katate dori ryote dori katate ryote dori	suwari waza tachi waza

(Source: http://www.aikikai.or.jp/eng/gradingsystem.htm)

9.4   The History of Aikido

The founder of Aikido, *o-sensei* Morihei Ueshiba was born on December 14, 1883 in Japan and died on April 26, 1969. He created Aikido as a synthesis of various martial arts that he had already learned as a youth. Particularly significant for its development was his association with a Master of the *"daito-ryu aikijutsu"* – Sokaku Takeda – who he met in about 1910 and with whom Morihei Ueshiba trained intensively for 3-4 years.

Besides his physical training, he was also interested in religion and spirituality. In this connection, a particular personality that Ueshiba met in 1919 has to be mentioned – Onisaburo Deguchi. Following the large changes that took place in the social order in Japan at the beginning of the 20th Century, numerous sects and religious communities emerged just as did the Deguchi *"omoto-kyo"* religion that at that moment could have counted several million followers.

Spirituality, as in the *"omoto-kyo"*, was perhaps one reason for Ueshiba's enlightening experience that he is supposed to have had in 1925, and which opened up the way to his 'discovery' of the 'secret of the universe'. Whatever is reported over this and whether it is true or not cannot be absolutely ascertained – some things that are written today over the life of Ueshiba rather belong to the annals of legend than the truth.

Nevertheless, Ueshiba's realization that the heart of martial arts *(Budo)* lay in unifying opposites and to respect current things and revere them. This gives us the basic thought in Aikido. Ueshiba first used the term 'Aikido' around 1925. He became even well known more with "his" martial art and in 1927 he went to Tokyo to give instruction there. Exercises with the sword and staff always belonged to the training program.

Around 1942, Ueshiba gradually pulled back from the limelight and handed over the directorship of his school – *hombu dojo* - to his son Kisshomaru Ueshiba (b. 1921 d. 1999).

After the Second World War, all martial arts were first of all, banned by the occupying American Forces. Instruction in Aikido could be first given 1949. In the decades that followed, Aikido eventually became known outside Japan, because numerous students of Morihei and Kisshomaru Ueshiba left Japan to spread Aikido round the world. Morihei Ueshiba, himself, only gave instruction to a few students in Iwama, Tokyo and various other towns.

Since the death of Kisshomaru Ueshiba, the current *doshu* (meaning approximately "Keeper of the Way") is Moriteru Ueshiba (b. 1951), the grandson of the founder. He continues his father's work. Kisshomaru Ueshiba restructured the *aiki-kai*, the well-known umbrella organization of Aikido (Aikikai Foundation founded 1948) and gave Aikido a systematic, modern form making it capable of being instructed and learned.

From today's viewpoint, Morihei Ueshiba is less the focal point of Aikido, but more the person who got an evolution going. This is the way that Aikido is instructed today across the world and it continues to increasingly win popularity, despite the fact that it does not have the public appeal of competition. For example, if you type the word 'Aikido' in any Internet search machine you will find well over 10 million results. On the large courses and seminars of well-known Masters of Aikido, you can meet *Aikido-ka* from many different nations and train alongside them.

Morihei Ueshiba

Some interesting dates:

- December 14, 1883: *O-sensei* Morihei Ueshiba born in Tanabe, Japan.

- 1903-1907: Enlisted into the Japanese Army and saw action in the Russo-Japanese war.

- 1910: Morihei Ueshiba meets Sokaku Takeda and learns *aiki-jutsu*; Settles in Hokkaido.

- 1919: Ueshiba makes acquaintance with Onisaburo Deguchi; Settles in Ayabe and does farming and studies *Budo*.

- June 27, 1921: Son Kisshomaru Ueshiba born in Ayabe.

- 1922: Ueshiba calls his martial art *aiki-bujutsu*.

- 1925: Around this time, Ueshiba calls his martial art Aikido.

- 1927: Ueshiba and his family move to Tokyo and he begins to instruct Aikido.

- 1930: Foundation of the *hombu dojo* in Tokyo.

- 1948: Foundation of the *Aikikai* Foundation.

- April 2, 1951: Birth of Moriteru Ueshiba – grandson of the Founder of Aikido.

- 1956: Kisshomaru Ueshiba begins to give Aikido instruction.

- 1957: Kisshomaru Ueshiba publishes his first Aikido book.

- April 26, 1969 Morihei Ueshiba dies at the age of 86.

- 1969: Kisshomaru Ueshiba is made *aikido-doshu*.

- 1975: Foundation of the International Aikido Federation (IAF).

- 1996: Moriteru Ueshiba made head of the *hombu dojo*.

- January 4, 1999 Kisshomaru Ueshiba dies at the age of 77.

- 1999: Moriteru Ueshiba is made *aikido-doshu*.

kamiza at the hombu dojo in Tokyo

One personality that has influenced Aikido since the 80s is Christian Tissier, *7th dan aikikai* (born 1951). After the Second World War, more and more foreigners came to Japan to learn Aikido from Kisshomaru and Moriteru Ueshiba in the *hombu dojo* as well as from many other teachers of the art. This included Christian Tissier who went to Japan in 1969 and trained intensively in Aikido there for seven years.

Christian Tissier had already begun to train in Aikido in 1962 in Paris and graduated to 2nd *dan* in 1968. In the *hombu dojo* in Tokyo, he trained for several hours every day under all the instructors teaching there at the time. Alongside this, he practiced *ken-jutsu* and kickboxing. In July 1976, he returned to Paris as a 4th *dan* and founded the now well-known "Cercle Christian Tissier" in Paris-Vincennes. Even after his long stay in Japan, he returned regularly to Tokyo to carry on learning Aikido from his instructors there. In 1998, he was awarded the 7th *dan aikikai* from the *doshu* at that time – Kisshomaru Ueshiba.

Besides Kisshomaru Ueshiba, there was another pupil of the founder of Aikido who had a large influence on Christian Tissier. This was Seigo Yamaguchi (b. 1924, d. 1996). It is thanks to Seigo Yamaguchi in particular that Aikido today exists in a well-thought out and dynamic form, because it was he who developed it considerably further.

By virtue of the history of Aikido, Japan is the country of its origin and logically you find there the traditional center of the sport – the *Aikikai* Foundation and the *hombu dojo*, in which the *doshu* Moriteru Ueshiba instructs. However, because of its worldwide popularity it is also liable to other cultural influences and has been or is being developed further in various directions according to the interests of its instructors. This is why, in the meanwhile, you will find a number of styles in Aikido that have all various foci.

Even during the lifetime of Morihei Ueshiba - founder of Aikido – Aikido did not exist in a uniform style. On the contrary, he was always developing his Aikido further and experimenting with various different movements. This is why you will see a variety of techniques in old photos and films of the founder.

In a small way, for the *Aikido-ka* this kind of development is what also happens today – as a beginner he moves quite differently than he would with 30 years of Aikido experience under his belt.

Accordingly, the *aikikai* formulates its perspective of the future in this way:

"As travel, work, and study abroad have now become commonplace, Aikido is spreading internationally because it can be viewed as a "product of a shared cultural heritage," culture not bound to any one nation or people a legacy which can contribute to peace and prosperity. Seen as such, expectations for Aikido's role in the coming century are great." *(Source: http://www.aikikai.or.jp/eng/aikikai.htm)*

Christian Tissier shihan, 7th dan 2007 during a summer seminar in Germany. Uke: Pascal Guillemin, 5th dan aikikai.

9.5   Tips for Beginners - FAQ

When you begin to learn Aikido, the key to success is continual training and practice. Straight away at the start, the plethora of techniques is confusing and, moreover, the *Aikido-ka* has not only to concentrate on himself but also on his counterpart. Therefore, it is important to train and practice regularly without too long a pause in between. One or two hours, two times a week is certainly sufficient for a good start in Aikido. Experience indicates that it is difficult at the beginning to have to concentrate on totally new movements for longer than an hour.

How Long Does it Take to Learn Aikido?

"How long does it take to learn Aikido?" is a question that every Aikido instructor has probably been asked at least once. The stock answer is simple: All life long! Because Aikido is a martial art and this inherently includes the search for the ideal movement, there will always be an aspect on which the *Aikido-ka* has to do more work. In connection with this, Aikido is easily comparable to other art forms like, for example, playing the piano or painting. These also have no conclusive point when one can say that you have reached the end completely.

Such an answer will be, of course, insufficient for a beginner. A better answer is to say that, on average, you need about 5-6 years to reach the grade of *shodan* (see Chapter 9.3). However, this is dependent on the frequency of training, previous personal experience, talent and last, but not least, your instructor. Above all, in order to learn Aikido, the student needs a lot of patience with himself and his training partner, because, in the main, Aikido techniques contain really complex sequences of movements. As mentioned before, the grading tests can help to increase the success of learning.

Can Aikido be Used in Self-defense?

Presumably, another question that every Aikido instructor has been asked at least once is whether Aikido functions in real situations. The basic answer to this is that Aikido is a martial art and a martial art that doesn't function in reality would be useless.

A more comprehensive answer to this question is similar to the previous one: Whether Aikido functions or not depends very much on the individual *Aikido-ka* – his prowess and his ability. If he doesn't succeed in defending himself in a real situation doesn't mean that Aikido as a martial art has failed, but rather that the person himself still did not posses the required ability.

This is no different to other martial art forms. If a *Karate-ka* fails to break a wooden plank while doing a breaking test, one would not say that it was *Karate* that didn't work – similarly if a boxer is knocked out it is the boxer's fault and not the sport of boxing.

However, it is certain that, generally, the focus of Aikido training is not about its functionality, but about learning an ideal technique (see Chapter 7.3).

Is Aikido a Form of Meditation?

An answer to this question presumes that the questioner and answerer understand meditation in the same way, because this word is often used very loosely in varying connections.

If meditation is taken to mean simply concentrated attentiveness then Aikido, as a martial art, certainly contains meditative elements. How, otherwise could one think of a martial art where you are not having to concentrate or remain attentive? This is why some people describe Aikido as "meditation in movement".

Concentrated attentiveness: Christian Tissier and Bodo Roedel – irimi nage.

If one understands meditation merely as a state of thinking back to oneself then Aikido completely transcends this idea, because the fascinating thing about Aikido is the process of communication with a counterpart.

In some books about the subject of Aikido and martial arts you will also find reference to *zen*. In *zen*, the accent is put on detachment from all things and on turning the eye inward. This is only applicable in a martial art as long as one retains freedom of action and can remain open and flexible. Otherwise, the student of a martial art form has at least the intention of defending himself. An additional aspect in Aikido is exactly learning self-assertion and determination of your movements.

Further Reading:
Deshimaru, T. (1992) *The Zen Way to Martial Arts: A Japanese Master Reveals the Secrets of the Samurai* (Penguin Paperback)

Herrigel, E. (1999) *Zen in the Art of Archery* (Vintage Paperback)

How Can I Find the Best dojo?

Those interested in Aikido and looking for a *dojo* should consider the following:

- You can learn Aikido in a club or in an Aikido school or academy. The latter often offer fuller and flexible training sessions and usually have a better layout and equipment.
- As can be expected, the standard of instruction, unfortunately, is often varied. Similarly, the fees or subscriptions and the level of *dan* grading of the instructor are not always an indicator of the quality. The latter is because a *dan* grading is awarded for lifetime or even for intra-organisation politics. Also, the standards of the grading tests for the *dan* level are often different from organization to organization.

- In the meanwhile, several different styles of Aikido have been developed that set a variety of different foci. So, you will find Aikido systems that are very static or that are similar to meditation (without movement) or gymnastics. Sometimes the *Aikikai*-mainstream of Aikido is difficult to discover in such cases.

It follows from these three points of view that on the one hand it is always sensible to compare various schools or clubs – to do this it is recommended to check for free introductory lessons that may be on offer. On the other hand, if you are going to be serious about your ambition to learn, then you should widen your horizon and look for weekend seminars with other Aikido instructors and other styles.

What is a Suitable Age to be Doing Aikido?

Whatever is valid for any movement form of sport is also valid for Aikido – the younger the better. Many *dojos* offer Aikido for kids to bring them slowly on to the main training. At the same time it is always a good thing to allow them to learn the motor system capability rather more in a playful form so that they have fun learning than trying to do serious practice with the difficult Aikido techniques.

Children also learn in martial arts to keep to the rules of the *dojo* as well as act with respect for others and be polite. They also exercise responsibility for themselves and others. Therefore, in instruction in Aikido with children it is not only about exercising the motor system, it has also to do with social behavior. Martial arts promote the build-up of self-confidence and self-assurance considerably – this is, of course, also valid for Aikido.

Because there is no competition in Aikido, men and women of all ages can practice together. It goes to say, therefore, that it is perfectly possible to begin doing Aikido at quite a mature age. This is also quite possible, because with age you can regulate the speed and intensity of the Aikido exercises well yourself. They promote the coordination of arm and leg movements and improve the performance and condition.

9.6   Information Sources

Books

By Kisshomaru Ueshiba
(1985) *Aikido* (Japan Publications Trading)
This is a basic textbook on Aikido by the son of the founder of Aikido.

(1988) *The Spirit of Aikido* (Kodansha International)
In this book the son of the Aikido founder devotes himself to the spiritual aspects of Aikido.

By Morihei Ueshiba
(1996) *Budo: Teachings of the Founder of Aikido* (Kodansha International)
Posthumous book written by the founder of Aikido.

By Moriteru Ueshiba
(2002) *Best Aikido: The Fundamentals* (Kodansha International)

(2003) *The Aikido Master Course: Best Aikido 2* (Kodansha International)

(2005) *Progressive Aikido: The Essential Elements* (Kodensha International)

By Christain Tissier
(1990) *Aikido* (Boulogne-Billancourt: Sedirep)
All the basic Aikido techniques (5th – 1st kyu) are shown in this book (text in French).

DVDs

Chr. Tissier: (2004) *AIKIDO Principes et Applications – Volume 1: Immobilisations.*

Chr. Tissier: (2004) *AIKIDO Principes et Applications – Volume 2: Projections.*

Chr. Tissier: (2007) *Variations et applications.*

Chr. Tissier: (2008) *An Aikido Odyssey*

Seigo Yamaguchi: (2009) *A Seminar in Paris.*

Internet Addresses

www.aikikai.or.jp
www.christiantissier.com
www.aiki.com
www.aikikai.org
www.aikido-world.com
www.aikidofaq.com
www.aikido-europe.com
www.aikido-international.org
www.aikido-schule.de

Association

International Aikido Federation (IAF)
c/o Aikikai Foundation
17-18 Wakamatsu-cho
Shinjuku-ku
Tokyo 162-0056 Japan
Tel. 082 – 2111271
Fax. 082 – 2111955
E-Mail: goldsbury@aikido-international.org
www.aikido-international.org

Photo and Illustration Credits

Cover Design:	Sabine Groten
Cover Photo:	Iris Pohl
p. 21, 323:	Photo of Morihei Ueshiba from: John Stevens „Unendlicher Friede", Kristkeitz Verlag. Reprinted with kind permission www.kristkeitz.de
p. 36:	from B. Roedel (2006), Richtig Aikido, BLV Verlag, p. 34
p. 272 bottom & p. 273 top:	from B. Roedel (2006), Richtig Aikido, BLV Verlag, pp. 50 and 51
p. 283:	from B. Roedel (2006), Aikido – Techniken, Angriffe und Bewegungseingänge, BLV Verlag, p. 122
	Reprinted with kind permission

For other photo credits see Page 14.

9.7 Glossary of Japanese Terms

Here we include a résumé of the more important Japanese terms used in Aikido. The translations are approximate and specific to Aikido.

AI	Joining, unifying, harmonizing
AIKIDO-KA	The person practicing/exercising in Aikido
AIKI-KAI	The Aikido worldwide umbrella organization
ARIGATO	Thank you
ASHI	Foot, leg
ASHI BARAI	Sweeping with the leg
ATEMI	A punching technique in Aikido to stop or immobilize the attacker momentarily
BATTO JUTSU	The art of drawing the sword (older form of IAIDO)
BO	(Long) Staff/Stick
BOJUTSU	Techniques using the staff
BOKKEN/BOKUTO	Wooden sword (Aikido exercise weapon)
BUDO	'The way of combat'
BUSHI	Warrior, Samurai
BUSHIDO	The BUSHI code of honor
CHUDAN	Middle area – i.e., abdomen (stomach) and solar plexus
CHUDAN TSUKI	A punch at the stomach
DAN	Grade Level (cf also KYU)
DE-AI	The moment of the first contact in a technique
DO	Way, method, lesson
DOJO	Traditional practice room
DOSHU	Highest representative of the martial art (currently Moriteru Ueshiba – grandson of the founder of Aikido)
DOZO	"Please...." (As in "Please come in" – "Please carry on" etc)
ERI	Lapel/Collar (of jacket)
GEDAN	Lower area – i.e., from the belt line downwards
KERI/GERI	Kick
(KEIKO) GI	Exercise uniform (Judo uniform)
GO NO KEIKO	A form of practice carried out firmly and with force
GYAKU	Reverse, opposite
GYAKUTE	Knife held in a stabbing position (e.g., as in SHOMEN or YOKOMEN UCHI)
GYAKU HANMI	Mirror-image position of feet of Uke and Tori

HAKAMA	A Japanese traditional pair of pants (culottes)
HANMI	Stance, posture, position
HARA	Stomach, center or middle of the body
HENKA	Change of posture, position without moving the feet
HENKA WAZA	A variation of a basic technique
HIDARI	Left
HIJI	Elbow
HO	Exercise, studying a principle (e.g., KOKYU HO)
HOMBU DOJO	The main DOJO of the AIKIKAI Foundation in which (amongst others) the DOSHU instructs
HONTE	Knife held in a cutting position
IAIDO	The art of drawing the sword
IAITO	Training sword in IAIDO
IKKYO	The first principle; the first teaching, first holding position
IRIMI	Moving straight in, entering
JIU WAZA	Free training
JO	Staff, stick (exercise weapon in Aikido)
JODAN	Upper area – i.e., head and neck
JU-JUTSU	Modern form of martial art based on the older method of JIU-JITSU
JU NO GEIKO	A soft form of exercising/practicing
KAI	Association, grouping, school – e.g., AIKI-KAI
KAITEN	Twisting movement
KAITEN NAGE	A twisting throw
KAMAI	The basic position – the on guard position
KAMIZA	Place of honor in the DOJO
KATA	Laid down form of movement - also 'shoulder'
KATAME WAZA	Pinning technique on the ground
KATANA	Japanese sword
KEIKO	Training, practice, revision
KEN	Sword
KENDO	Japanese fencing
KENJUTSU	Fighting technique using the sword
KESA GIRI	Diagonal cut
KI	Spirit, purpose, energy, feeling
KIAI	Cry to mobilize the KI
KIHON	Basic
KI MUSUBI	Tying-in with the partner's KI. (The process of matching one's partner's movement)

KOKORO	Heart, mind, mentality
KOKYU	Breathing, Exchange
KOKYU-HO	Exercising the principle of KOKYU
KOSHI	Hip
KOSHI NAGE	Hip throw
KOTE	Wrist
KOTE-GAESHI	Throw executed with a wrist turn or twist
KUBI	Neck
KUMI-TACHI	Partners exercising with a sword
KUMI JO	Partners exercising with the stick
KYU	Belt grade (prior to DAN)
KYUDO	The way of archery
MA	Distance
MA-AI	Correct distance
MAE	Frontal
MAE GERI	Forward kick
MAWASHI GERI	Roundhouse kick (circular kick)
MIGI	Right
MUNE	Chest
MUNE DORI	Grasping the lapel (of jacket)
NAGE	The person who executes the technique (also TORI or SHITE)
NAGE WAZA	Throwing technique
OMOTE	Front/forward
ONEGAI SHIMASU	Sentence spoken for greeting, lit. 'Please'.
OSAE WAZA	Holding or pinning technique e.g., IKKYO
O-SENSEI	Literally 'Great Master' – title of respect given to Morihei Ueshiba
RANDORI	Free exercise, defense against a number of attackers
REI	Bow
REIGI	Etiquette, rules of behavior in the DOJO
RYU	School for martial arts
SEIZA	Sitting on the heels, formal sitting position
SENSEI	Teacher, instructor or person warranting respect
SHIHAN	Master instructor, lit. 'model'
SHIHO GIRI	Cutting (with hand, knife or sword) in four directions – SHI = 4
SHIHO NAGE	A 'four-directions' throw
SHIKKO	Moving/walking on the knees
SHIN	Heart, mind, spirit
SHISEI	Correct posture

SHIZENTAI	Natural/normal stance or posture
SHODAN	1st DAN (SHO = one, to begin, to start) − i.e., SHODAN is where you are at the beginning of Aikido
SHOMEN	Front (as in 'front of head')
SODE	Sleeve (of jacket)
SOKUMEN	Diagonal, to one side (also NANAME)
SOTO	Outside
SUMO	Japanese wrestling
TAI	Body
TAI NO HENKA	Twist/turn of the hips without changing the position of the legs/feet.
TAI SABAKI	Body movement (often in combination with IRIMI-TENKAN)
TAISO	Gymnastics, warm-up training
TANTO DORI	Techniques against knife attacks
TATAMI	Mats
TE	Hand
TE-GATANA	Using the hand like a sword - with the side of the hand acting as the edge
TENCHI NAGE	Heaven (TEN) and earth (CHI) throw
TENKAN	Turn, pivoting movement on the foot in order to dodge
TSUGI ASHI	Gliding step (usually done without changing the leg)
TSUKI	Punch with the fist
UCHI	Inside, striking, punching
UDE	Arm
UDE KIME NAGE	Arm lock throw
UKE	The person who attacks and is thrown
UKEMI	Fall, breakfall
URA	The rear side, back
USHIRO	Behind, to the rear, backwards
WAZA	Technique
YARI	Lance
YOKO	Side
YOKOMEN	Side of the head
YUDANSHA	Black belt or DAN holder
ZANSHIN	Maintaining attentiveness at the end of a technique
ZAREI	Bowing from a kneeling position
ZORI	Japanese sandals

Japanese Numbers

1	ICHI	6	ROKU
2	NI	7	SHICHI or NANA
3	SAN	8	HACHI
4	SHI or YON	9	KYU or KU
5	GO	10	JU

9.8   Index

If you have any comments or can recommend improvements to this book, then please send a letter or email to the Author.

Aikido-Schule Bodo Roedel
Lichtstrasse 38
50825 Cologne
Germany
Tel: +49-(0)221-546 1313
Email: info@aikido-schule.de
Internet: www.aikido-schule.de

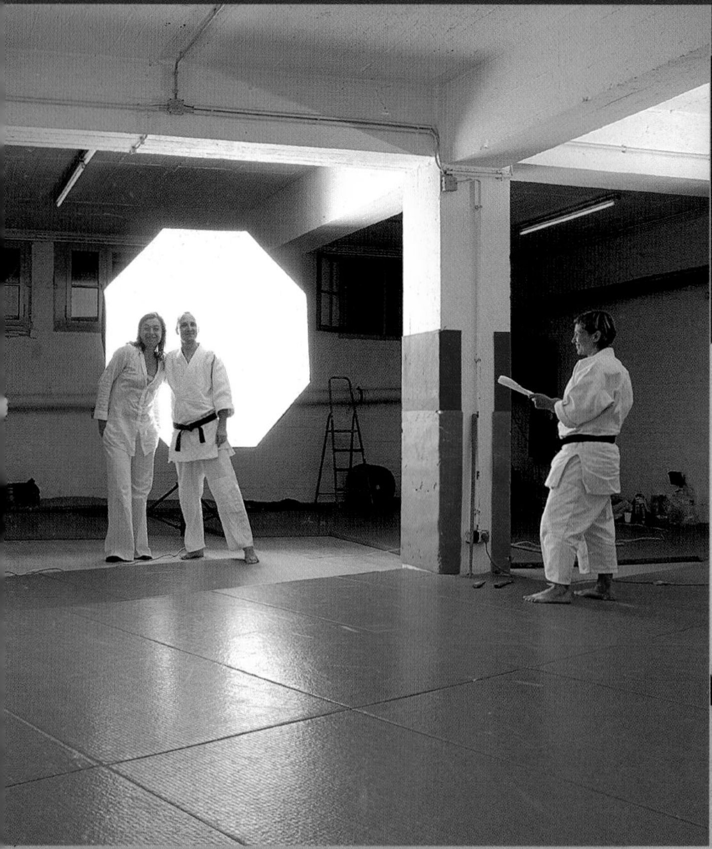

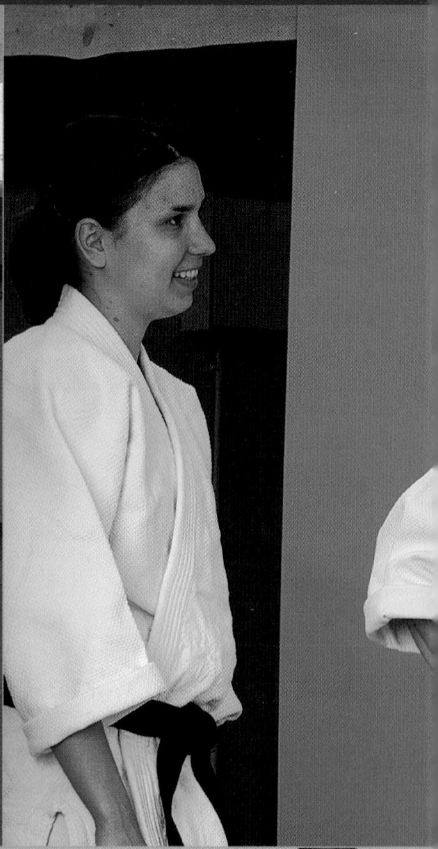

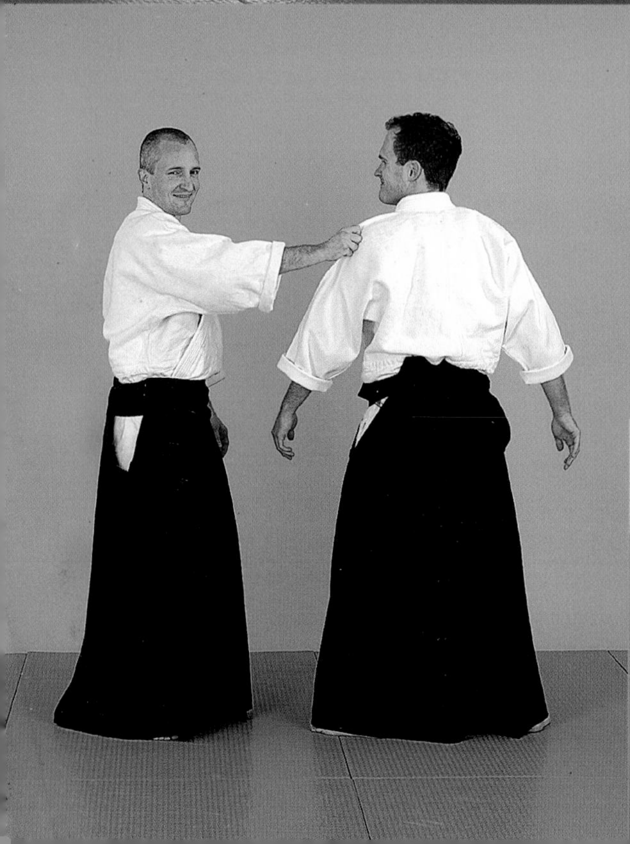

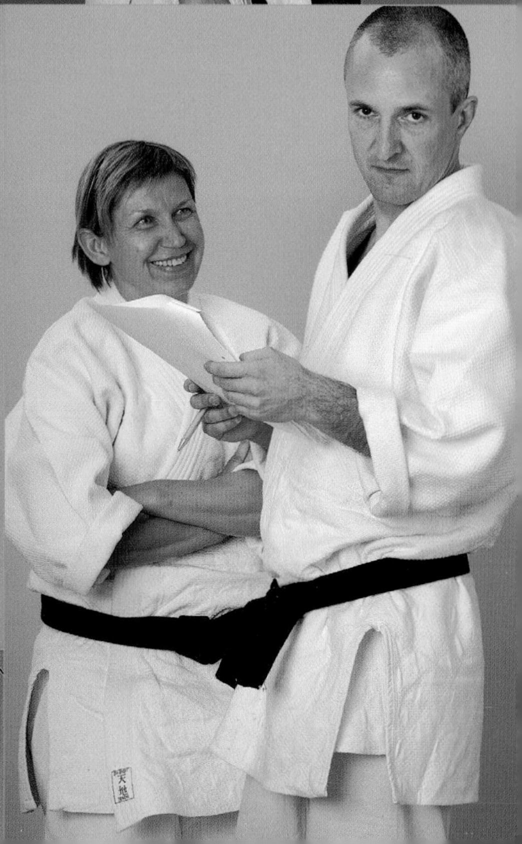